Cohen, Jeffrey H.

Cultures of migration

CULTURES OF MIGRATION

Cultures of Migration

THE GLOBAL NATURE OF
CONTEMPORARY MOBILITY

Jeffrey H. Cohen and Ibrahim Sirkeci

UNIVERSITY OF TEXAS PRESS
Austin

Requests for permission to reproduce material from this work should
be sent to:
    Permissions
    University of Texas Press
    P.O. Box 7819
    Austin, TX 78713-7819
    www.utexas.edu/utpress/about/bpermission.html

∞ The paper used in this book meets the minimum requirements of
ANSI/NISO z39.48-1992 (R1997) (Permanence of Paper).

LIBRARY OF CONGRESS CATALOGING-IN-PUBLICATION DATA
Cohen, Jeffrey H. (Jeffrey Harris)
Cultures of migration : the global nature of contemporary
mobility / Jeffrey H. Cohen and Ibrahim Sirkeci.
        p.   cm.
Includes bibliographical references and index.
ISBN 978-0-292-72684-0 (cloth : alk. paper)
ISBN 978-0-292-72685-7 (pbk. : alk. paper)
ISBN 978-0-292-73536-7 (E-book)
    1. Emigration and immigration—Social aspects.   2. Emigration
and immigration—Economic aspects.   I. Sirkeci, Ibrahim.
II. Title.
JV6225.C64   2011
304.8—dc22
                                                2011001178

For movers and their families

CONTENTS

PREFACE

This book began as a discussion between Cohen and Sirkeci regarding the meaning of migration. We started by email, talking about our work. Cohen had spent several years looking at the patterns of migration in rural southern Mexico, while Sirkeci had done the same in the Kurdish parts of Turkey. Later, we shared papers and began to compare the outcomes we had noted in these populations. Sirkeci also began *Migration Letters*, a journal focused on migration research from around the globe, and he invited Cohen to join him as co-editor. Our work with the many authors contributing to *Migration Letters*, as well as our ongoing investigations in two similar fields—anthropology and geography—suggested to us that there were strong parallel currents between the migration experiences of very different populations.

The parallels in the patterns and processes we discovered among Mexican and Kurdish migrations have fueled an ongoing conversation about the meaning, scope, and outcomes of human mobility. Our work here is a part of that conversation, an attempt to frame migration in a way that builds upon earlier work but that also lays out what we see as a new foundation for continued analysis and debate. Specifically, we develop a cultural framework, or *a culture of migration*, that acknowledges the various ways in which migration decisions are made and that demonstrates how individual decisions are rooted in the social practices and cultural beliefs of a population.

Put another way, we argue that the choice to migrate is not driven by economic need alone, nor is a desire to leave a natal home a sufficient catalyst for border crossing. Culture—in other words, the social practice, meaning, and symbolic logic of mobility—must be understood along with economics if we are to understand patterns of migration. We are certainly not alone in our belief that economics on its own is not an adequate explanation. This is widely accepted in migration literature. Thomas Faist

(2000a:17) describes the challenge facing migration research as the need to understand the meso-level effects of mobility, or the outcomes that take place in the social universe of the mover. Faist's approach contrasts with micro-level analyses that focus on the psychology of the migrant and the desires, drives, and practices of movers (Bougue 1977; Douglass 1970; Gamio 1969; Koch 1989; Mahler 1995), on the one hand, and, on the other, macro-level analyses that define migration for a nation and a region (Taylor et al. 1996).

Our focus on the meso-level is important for better understanding how migrants talk about and frame their experiences. Nevertheless, the decision to migrate is a profoundly personal one, and it reflects individual strengths and desires. Migrants make their sojourns to better themselves, to satisfy needs, and to care for their families and homes. They also migrate to escape undesirable conditions. For example, many Mexican women migrate to escape familial violence, turning their backs on homes and parents in an effort to find a safer environment in which to live. Kurds in the Middle East and many groups in Iraq also flee their homelands not simply to find prosperity, but to escape insecurity brought on by ongoing conflicts within these areas (Sirkeci 2005, 2006a, 2006b). Even the North African who is seeking economic opportunities unavailable at home moves for social, cultural, and political as well as economic reasons (Castles 2009).

A focus on the migrant—or a micro-level analysis—runs the risk of ignoring macro-level as well as meso-level outcomes. First, while sojourns are personal decisions, they are also typically decisions made in response to economic troubles at home, social processes at home and abroad, and judgments concerning treatment abroad. Second, understanding the push and pull of local economic life and how local political ways frame the migrant's negotiation of security is critical to understanding migration outcomes. Third, decisions are always bigger than the individuals involved. For example, personal choice does not fully explain why Filipinos are driven to join nursing programs and train to become caregivers in the United States. The reality is that children who join the program often do so in response to the insistence and direction of their parents (Kingma 2005).

In a similar fashion, macro-level analyses that are focused on the national or global economic and political forces that drive migration outcomes do not account for social and cultural practices that can increase border crossing or sometimes check migration patterns. What do we mean? Think about a typical Mexican migrant from the state of Oaxaca's central valleys, the site of most of Cohen's studies. Oaxacan migrants to the U.S. are young men, and typically they migrate to support families and their households. Women are not well represented in the Oaxacan migrant stream to the U.S., yet when it comes to internal moves, women and men travel at nearly the same rate (Cohen, Rodriguez, and Fox 2008). To understand this pattern, we must look beyond macro-level forces (in fact, at a national level, Mexican women outnumber men as movers to the U.S.) and toward cultural beliefs and social patterns that influence migration decision–making. Following traditional Oaxacan beliefs, women should not migrate to the U.S. Oaxacans believe that women belong at home caring for families. This set of beliefs, as well as fear of sending women alone to unknown places, limits the percentage of women who cross the border in search of work in the U.S.

Our analysis of the social and cultural basis of migration is not meant to replace micro- or macro-level understandings of mobility. Instead our goal is to introduce a complementary model of movement that focuses on social practices and patterns and cultural beliefs even as we recognize migration's economic and political drives. Again, our goal is to add to the debate on human movement and to suggest that a culture of migration exists in nearly all migrant and refugee settings. Cultural traditions and practices frame, reframe, and finally form responses and outcomes that allow people to make sense of what is going on around them (and see Bourdieu 1977 on the concept of *habitus*). It is our hope that this approach, which brings together anthropological and geographic sensibilities as well as sociological and economic models, can help advance our understanding of migration and mobility outcomes.

The study of migration is an important current in our fields, and while its roots may be somewhat deeper in geography, understanding why and how people move is critical to both the anthropologist and the geographer. At the same time, we believe there is a renewed urgency to studying and understanding migration. Too often, migration is misunderstood as something that challenges the cultural fabric of a society and disrupts social and economic life. In fact, migration is simply movement, nothing more or less. Humans, like many other animals in this world, migrate. And while prehistoric movement lies beyond the scope of our inquiry, our very evolution as a species is linked to our ability to move and adapt to new environments (on early human migration and settlement see Cavalli-Sforza and Cavalli-Sforza 1995). In the contemporary world many humans continue to migrate annually. Some migrations are motivated by an urge to escape a situation, and sometimes migration is nothing more than the need to escape colder winters, such as the Englishmen who crowd the beaches of southern Europe. Others move to seek temporary or seasonal employment and supplement low incomes and limited opportunities; here, we can think of the migrants that Cohen studies in southern Mexico.

Anthropology is replete with stories of pastoralists as well as pilgrims — both are in a sense migrating groups of people, different in quality, but at their core movers (Massey et al. 1998). Yet at present contemporary migration is often seen as something unique, new, and often threatening. And while some migrants travel freely and others are refugees, we should not assume that migrants have no home and that they seek to displace others. The reality is far from this dangerous caricature. Migrants are people who move — some move for reasons of employment, others for reasons of pleasure. Some seek to escape from something — fear and a lack of security — while others seek to find something — stability and belonging. Understanding these patterns is critical and our goal.

This book then is meant as one phase in the continued dialogue between the fields of anthropology and geography, which is also a dialogue about places and people. Unlike the work we have both done as individuals, this book brings examples together from many different parts of the globe. We follow people who are moving from the west to the east and from the south to the north. Our examples include Mexicans and Turks, but also people from Europe, sub-Saharan Africa, the Pacific, and many parts of Asia. Our goal is to show the cultural basis of this movement and the human dimensions of global mobility. We do not purport to have all of the answers, nor can we cover all of the examples of migration. Nevertheless, we believe our contribution is an important one that builds upon work in the social sciences and defines a new path to understanding the culture of migration.

ACKNOWLEDGMENTS

Co-authoring is always a difficult process; nevertheless, it is one with a great payoff. It allows researchers to share approaches and it creates an opportunity to critically engage theories that aren't always apparent. Our setting, one that bridges anthropological and geographic models of migration and brings complementary ethnographic examples to the fore, has given us an opportunity to write what we believe is a unique book on international migration, bringing together different disciplinary perspectives and questioning the role of conflicts, insecurity, economic motives, transnationalism, and sociocultural influences at the micro-, meso-, and macro-levels by drawing upon examples from around the world.

Our relationship has developed over many years, during which we have shared our work—Cohen on Mexico and specifically Oaxacan migration patterns as well as the experiences of Dominicans in new receiving communities; Sirkeci on Turkey and the experiences of Turkish Kurds in Western Europe as well as outcomes of migration in the face of violence for Iraqis. This has been a rewarding relationship, and we are both surprised by the similarities we find among Oaxacan and Kurdish migrants. In fact, our first joint effort compared migration outcomes for Oaxacans and Kurds (Cohen and Sirkeci 2005).

This project grows from our belief that the study of migration too often ignores cultural outcomes and social forces that influence migration and remittance practices. We found that most discussions of migration typically focused on the economic factors driving migration and the social costs of migration for sending and receiving communities. We also realized that, with the exception of a few anthropologists and geographers, most analyses of migration outcomes tended to focus on receiving communities and countries and the actions of migrants as movers. We were left asking first, what are the effects of migration for sending households? And second, why don't more people migrate? Our questions were framed by patterns of household decision-making and a belief that migration was a cultural or social process, not merely a response to economic pressures at home and opportunities afar. We typically asked one another such questions as why would a Kurd stay in Iraq and choose to remain at home with his or her family when jobs are available in Germany, and why would a Mexican choose to stay in his or her rural hometown and not migrate across the border to the U.S. and opportunities and salaries that allow a worker to earn a day's wage in less than an hour.

There were plenty of other questions that gave us pause. Why it is that migration tends to flow south to north, east to west? The question may seem simple, and one potential answer follows the musings of Bill Clinton, who argued, "It's the economy, stupid." But if economics explained migration, it would be much easier to plan a response and organize to reduce the rate of border crossing.

We dedicate this work not to one person, but to the millions of movers who migrate so that they can provide for their families and homes. They are the unseen, the unknown. They should not be criticized for their actions; rather, we need to better understand why they move, so that we might better help them and the countries they travel to better respond to and accommodate these patterns. We are grateful to hundreds of respondents who have helped in our own research but also to the hundreds of others we have quoted from other studies.

We are grateful to our families for their support and for giving us the time to complete this book. We also thank our friends, the National Science Foundation Program in Cultural Anthropology, and our colleagues who have commented on this work at earlier stages as well as the anonymous reviewers whose constructive comments helped us to enhance this work.

Introduction THE CULTURES OF MIGRATION

Hey you, you think I'm mojado? *You're the* mojado!
My family has been here forever. . . . Your families!
Your families came here in a boat!
—DON MARIO, OAXACA, MEXICO, 1993,
IN A HEATED DISCUSSION WITH COHEN

Lots of people talk about migration and lots of people talk about migrants. They are intrigued by the process and they want to ask questions about why people move. Many people assume migrants are seeking to escape something that cannot be resolved in their home country. Others figure that migration is a solution to a local economic problem such as the lack of jobs. When a country cannot provide for its citizens, those citizens may choose to migrate to a country where opportunities are present (Goodman and Hiskey 2008). The belief that migration is an important option for people who cannot make a living in their native homes can often promote a fearful reaction among receiving populations. They oppose migration in general and assume that migrants are people who take jobs, bring crime, and access services that are better held for the native-born. Ultimately these assumptions about migration can and often do lead to xenophobia, especially in times of economic crisis. Xenophobic reactions include fear of both migration and migrants as well as the belief that migrants bring with them culture and practices that challenge and threaten the fabric of the destination nation's traditional way of life.[1]

Discussions of migration and the migrant, of the movements of populations from south to north, east to west, poor to rich, and insecurity toward security fill library shelves. But how should we talk about migration? It isn't accurate to regard migration as something new and unique. Migration is a historical process, and it has been around for a long time. While contemporary movements might seem extraordinary, the phenomenon shares

a lot with what has happened before (Massey et al. 1998). Just as importantly, migration is not a solitary process. It isn't just about a mover and
where he or she goes. Migration is about security and escaping dangerous
situations. It is about the sending households that are homes to migrants
and about the communities where those households are found. Migration
is local and follows individual movers to internal destinations. It is also
about international flow and global processes. We must look beyond the
present and the person to understand the history and sociocultural setting
of the mover.

Our goal is to frame migration in ways that allow it to be better understood. We want to capture the growth in migration literature and interest in migration among policy makers, academics, and the public, using
anthropology, demography, and geography to explain at least a bit of what
is going on. Our intent is to clarify definitions and enhance understanding
of this complex phenomenon. We aim to continue (not resolve) the debate
on the definition and meaning of migration, the dynamic nature of human
mobility, the place and role that security plays in movement, and the culture of migration cultivated, created, and recreated through the process of
migration.

Our definition of migration is rooted in an understanding of the household as the adaptive unit where social actors make active decisions (Wilk
1991). In other words, migrants do not act alone. They come to their decisions in discussions with other members of their households and with
friends and relatives at points of origin and destination. Although sometimes they ignore the household, and sometimes the household over-
whelms the mover, the household is always present, regardless of the
situation therein. Beyond the household, the decision to migrate reflects
communal traditions, village practices, and national or even international
trends.

A critical factor in the discussions concerning migration is security.
We have no problem assuming that migrants leave their homes in search
of work and economic security. But we also want to push this concept
forward and argue that security is more than an economic outcome. It is
cultural as well as social. Migrants think about their well-being and their
security as individuals as well as members of culture groups and societies.
In other words, they are cultural agents and their decisions reflect larger
cultural and social debates. Migrants seek to live well, and this means they
consider cultural, economic, and social security in their decisions. They
want an opportunity to survive and thrive and to practice their culture in
a safe environment. They are also thinking about insecurity—what is lack-

ing at home that might motivate their moves. When we talk about refugees we assume they make their migrations happen in response to insecurity, whether political, religious, or environmental. But we argue that most migrants, regardless of their status, are thinking about issues of both security and insecurity in their decisions.

There is much debate and controversy surrounding the structure and meaning of migration. Therefore we start with a basic definition of migration. In later parts of this text we examine households, conflicts, and the culture of migration in detail. We also look into nonmovers, those left behind, who are crucial to understanding transnational mobility and the importance of the household in changing patterns of mobility and a conflict framework.

FRAMING MIGRATION

A 2006 United Nations General Assembly report noted that globally nearly 200 million people were involved in one or another form of international migration (2006).[2] In other words, the movement between two sovereign nations by sojourners, asylum seekers, refugees, and the like includes literally millions of individuals on a yearly basis. Yet the United Nations' numbers do not include internal migrants (those movers who choose to remain within a nation's boundaries) nor do they include internally displaced persons who cannot or will not leave their country of origin.[3]

Despite being criticized by researchers and practitioners as employing too broad a definition to be useful, the U.N.'s model of migration—defined as individuals who live away from their place of origin for at least a year— has been widely adopted by academics and policy makers, and most available statistics have been collected accordingly. The "length of absence" criteria (i.e., those who migrated went to another country for more than twelve months) complicate understanding migration and make it difficult to develop a complete and complex picture of international movement.[4] Defining migration as something that must last for at least a year leaves uncounted the millions of people who move for only a short period of time, and those individuals who cross borders regularly yet return nightly to their sending home. This last group includes those movers who live in the border areas, or "borderland people" (Horstmann and Wadley 2006). Groups in border areas often move daily across international boundaries, yet because they are permanent residents in their county of origin, they are not, by definition, "migrants." Not obvious as migrants or migrations in such restrictive lenses are the daily trips or circular and seasonal migrations made by Mexicans crossing the U.S. border, Polish movers who commute to nearby German towns, Laotians who are working across the border in Thailand factories, or Turks, Arabs, and Kurds[5] who regularly cross the southeastern border between Turkey, Iraq, and Syria for trade, funerals, weddings, and the like. Nevertheless, these movements are voluminous and are part of the growth, history, and culture of migration.

Alongside these temporary and local short-term sojourners are other mobile populations who often do not show up in migration registers. Foreign students (Scheurle and Seydel 2000), holiday makers, professionals, and business people who spend a significant portion of their time away from their homelands are all migrants of a sort who do not "count" in estimates of international movers. Academics are another example of migrants, as they may spend lengthy periods abroad teaching or conducting research.

Can we call these diverse groups migrants? It may seem odd, but there are studies of holiday movers (Buckley 2005; Kinnaird 1999), nostalgic travelers (Vryer 1989), religious pilgrims (Brower 1996; Leppakari 2008; Moerman and Collcutt 2008), and highly skilled, itinerant workers (Luthra 2009; Regets 2008), who are all often best described as migrants. The differences between these movers and refugees, forced migrants, displaced peoples, and even unskilled international movers are stark. While the religious pilgrim travels to her or his destination as a personal sacrifice to a belief, the refugee is moving in response to external and often uncontrolled outcomes. The unskilled migrant who leaves a rural home to find work might serve a highly skilled migrant from his home country in a restaurant, but he or she has little in common with the experience of this conational beyond place of birth. Zlolniski (2006) explores this process and the role that unskilled migrant labor serves in the support of highly skilled native and migrant labor in his work with Mexican immigrants to the Silicon Valley in central California. While highly skilled workers assimilate into middle-class America and upward mobility, most Mexican migrants to the region join the ranks of unskilled labor and face a future of downward mobility (and see the discussion of segmented assimilation in Waldinger and Lichter 2003).

The difference between these groups of migrants—the traveler, skilled mover, and religious pilgrim on the one hand and the unskilled migrant, refugee, and forced mover on the other—rests in the asymmetrical relationships the latter have with systems of power at points of origin and destination. The "weary, world traveler" fits into a prestigious slot in most countries and is encouraged to continue his or her tour. The religious pilgrim is celebrated and welcomed as a guest, and the highly skilled migrant fills an important niche in a nation's intellectual endeavors even as he or she shares a basic set of progressive beliefs (Cornelius, Espenshade, and Salehyan 2001). The unskilled migrant, the refugee, and the forced mover are not equals, regardless of their origin or destination: refugees are a burden, forced movers are a reminder of failed promises, and unskilled migrants are often seen as a nuisance even as they are encouraged to take low-wage positions with few benefits.

The asymmetrical relationships and social inequalities that characterize mobile populations and their relationships often contribute to a migrant's choice of destination; while these phenomena were noted in the 1970s by Eric Wolf (1972), among others, they are often overlooked in contemporary discussions of migration. This asymmetry can be geographic, economic, or social. Geographic asymmetry is evidenced when international moves bring fewer changes and complications than do internal moves. For example, while it is considered to be international migration when people migrate from Luxembourg to neighboring Belgium, moves between Xinjiang (or East Turkistan) and Shanghai in China are described as internal migrations. The international move from Luxembourg to Belgium involves almost no change in cultural, linguistic, socioeconomic, and legal environment. Yet the move within China represents an internal move from west to east, and includes a shift from a rural to an urban setting, and a change in language, economics, religion, and culture, not to mention the distance between the two regions. Shanghai is a densely populated global economic powerhouse with a dominant Chinese population while Xinjiang remains a rural, underdeveloped region ethnically dominated by the Uighurs, who suffer from internal discrimination in the People's Republic of China.[6]

A different asymmetry is evident when we consider migrations that are limited by the economic and social facilities of the movers in question; these are determined by the migrant's household and country, and the community's relationship to national and global processes. Wealthier households can afford to support longer moves and are usually able to send their members across national borders to access jobs and opportunities that are not available locally and that may take some time to find. Internal and regional movers are often members of lower economic classes, individuals whose households cannot afford the costs of crossing international borders (Carton de Grammont and Lara Flores 2010). These migrants do not have resources to support their moves across borders, nor do they have the time necessary to access distant opportunities. Many Central and South African movers fall into this latter group. They migrate regionally, from rural to urban setting, following social networks as they move from one part of the informal economy to another. Their earnings remain low and they find only limited opportunities, yet at the same time they are reducing the burden on their family and sending household (Cliggett 2003).

Cultural and social inequalities also create asymmetries for different movers and between movers and their destinations. Asymmetries can be gender based and define where men and women can and cannot travel. Asymmetries are also rooted in ethnic and religious differences that are expressed in opportunities or their lack when migrants determine destinations and must confront a religious system that is skeptical of their native beliefs. Such is the case in Canada and Britain, where Hindus, Sikhs, and Muslims encounter a Christian system that defines them as nonbelievers and potentially dangerous interlopers (Model and Lin 2002). Social and cultural differences can also affect whether a migrant makes a decision by choice or is forced to do so. In many countries, women are prohibited from making international moves—instead, women stay at home or move locally and when they do move internationally, they follow fathers and brothers (see Cohen, Rodriguez, and Fox 2008).

Ethnic and religious differences also impact migration outcomes. Ethnic and religious compatriots can be an important resource for the mover. He or she finds shelter, support, and a shared set of beliefs and practices that do not have to be explained. On the other hand, people of different faiths may greet migrants with skepticism and contempt. This is often the case whether ethnic minorities seek refuge in other countries or in regions within a country, and especially when differing belief systems encounter each other.

Where Christians and Muslims clash in the homeland, migration may be an important avenue for avoiding conflict, yet the religious nature of the clash can make movement difficult. Faith, like a label, marks the mover and restricts mobility as well as ability. In these situations, the members of the minority faith must move without the knowledge of the leaders of the dominant faith. And often the result is that the followers of minority faiths become refugees, as is currently the case in both Darfur and East Timor, two regions where religious differences have forced the large-scale movement of people and transformed them from citizens to refugees (Ferguson 2010; Ondiak and Ismail 2009; Wise 2006).

FROM MIGRATION TO MOBILITY

"Mobility" is a term that can be used to replace "migration" and help us explain and understand cross-border human movements. The advantages that come with using "mobility" in place of "migration" are twofold. First, "mobility" accommodates human movement beyond the limited definition of "migration," which is based on a twelve-month residence in a country that is foreign to the home country of the mover. Second, "mobility" is a dynamic term that emphasizes the changing, floating, fluid nature of this phenomenon and captures the regular as well as irregular moves of people on the ground regardless of time or destination.

Anthropologists, geographers, and other social scientists have long emphasized the importance of defining migration as a process that is regular and predictable. In other words, the motivations and the pathway to a destination are understandable. So too are the processes that promote migration as well as the outcomes that occur as migrants arrive at their destinations (for historical models see Ravenstein 1889; Zelinsky 1971).

Conceiving migration as mobility helps to define the process of movement and emphasizes its fluid progression even as it organizes a framework for understanding. Mobility breaks the conventional and static definition of migration offered by groups like the U.N. ("movement from point A to point B for at least 12 months") and more clearly defines it in relation to the experiences of movers and nonmovers as well as our experiences as researchers. It is abundantly clear that people travel not only to international destinations, but also to local destinations. The duration of their moves can range from short term, lasting for a few days, to long term, extending over many years. Finally, moves between more than two places are often typical for migrants; such multiple moves and circular moves are overlooked in the assumption that migration is unidirectional, beginning in country A ending in country B and lasting for at least a twelve-month period.

TRANSNATIONALISM

"Transnational movement" describes the circular movements of individuals and groups as they travel between two or more destinations in a regular fashion over time. Anthropologists among others use the term to describe migrations as mobile, cultural, and motivated by a variety of causes but also to contrast with the assumption that movement is typically from point A to point B, with little or no return or integration across space and time (Glick Schiller, Basch, and Blanc-Szanton 1992).

Transnationalism as an approach overcomes some of the ills of conventional views of migration—particularly the idea that movement follows one direction—and it embraces the view that migration is dynamic, multilocational, and circular as well as a natural part of human culture (Basch, Glick Schiller, and Blanc 1994). Any attempt to reconceptualize and redefine migration as a process must integrate a transnational perspective.

The concepts of transnationalism and the circular movement of individuals between two or more locations over time that often follows the back-and-forth, give-and-take interactions between a sending and a destination community are celebrated in the anthropological literature for the positive ways in which they create new space (often referred to as transnational space; see Pries 1999) for the construction of cultural, social and sometimes political identities (Kearney 1996). This process is evident in the ways that indigenous migrants from southern Mexico travel to Los Angeles, California, for work. In their new destination communities in southern California they forge an identity built around their indigenous, Mexican past, and are energized by a shared sense of identity that in turn becomes a foundation from which they demand political inclusion in their sending country (Rivera-Salgado 2000).

While celebrated for the ways it builds networks and revitalizes culture, transnationalism also brings with it certain costs; a recent special issue of *Migration Letters* focuses on these issues specifically (volume 6, no. 1 [April 2009]). The costs of transnationalism can be economic and include the expense of moving in a circular fashion. Importantly, transnational migration brings global economic ideals to rural communities, and the impact of these ideas and ideals is not simple. Transnational practices can create new stresses and place pressures on traditional practices that appear unworkable or problematic (Marcelli and Lindsay Lowell 2005). Socially, transnational migration reorganizes sending communities and introduces debates over the meaning of tradition. Movers do not leave, but rather rethink and redefine their roles, and nonmigrants or nonmovers may not be particularly supportive.

The transnational is just one kind of movement that can be critical to a mover's success. But how long do transnational migrations take? And how long does transnationalism last? These are complex questions, as many transnational movers transcend borders regularly and transnational practices come and go through time (see, for example, Guarnizo 1997).

To return to the idea of migration, the numbers provided by various supranational or national agencies can tell us only who is migrating in a given year, and even then count only those who stay twelve months or more. These numbers do not address questions such as how long a migrant may be absent from his and her home community, how many sojourns he or she has been involved in, and if the migrant who is currently in her or his destination country plans to return to his or her country and home of origin in the future. These data also lack any notion of transnationalism. Thus, as we have pointed out, these estimates of migration are problematic at best, particularly if we are interested in determining transnational outcomes (Cohen et al. 2003). They likely overlook many millions of undocumented movers who remain uncounted or do not want to be counted, as well as, among others, internal movers.

Regardless of the strength of the U.N.'s estimates, the numbers and patterns of movement they note remind us that people are moving in increasingly larger numbers from east to west and south to north, and not always to destinations in developed countries. Of course, over the last several decades the increase in the total number of migrants has risen rapidly. And while the numbers from the U.N. are indicative of global patterns of movement and the growth of that movement in demographic terms, they tell us little about the motivations behind migration; the concerns movers have about both security and insecurity; and how they migrate and the outcomes (or ends, if you will) of migration.

When we claim that there are many more millions of people globally involved in mobility (internal, transnational, and otherwise) than are normally tallied, we are not arguing for the inclusion of a perfect estimate of illegal or undocumented migrants, whose numbers are hard to define. Just to clarify how complicated mobility can become, we ask that you consider this: taking a look at the number of passengers departing or arriving at main global airports, we find a very complex picture. For the five airports in London, there is a total of over 200 million passengers passing through per annum. Add the totals for New York, Los Angeles, Paris, Shanghai, Beijing, Frankfurt, Moscow, Mexico City, and Istanbul, and the number of people moving—regardless of their status—becomes enormous. Of course we do not want to claim that all of the passengers identified within these airports are migrants, but they are mobile and, as we noted above, they might fall into one of the less common types of migrations we have identified (religious pilgrim, nostalgic traveler, or highly skilled worker). Some of these movers will settle; others will remigrate, relocate, or return;

and others will build upon strong social networks to create transnational spaces. Yet even a fraction of this total dwarfs the U.N.'s overall figures for migration.

CONFLICT AND MIGRATION
AND CONFLICT MIGRATION

Even as migrants plan their sojourns, balance family against self-interest, and gain at least some satisfaction from exercising their mobility, they are also sometimes challenged by internal conflicts, which can come in many forms, including ethnic or religious disputes; in their destinations they may face xenophobic responses to their moves. Internal disputes and anti-migration sentiments in destination countries are just two aspects of the conflicts we must acknowledge and take into account as dynamic building blocks of an improved understanding of transnational mobility.

Our definition of conflict builds upon the work of Ralf Dahrendorf (1959). Dahrendorf argued that "conflict" is not necessarily equal to "violence": it embraces a range of situations from latent tensions to violent encounters. Conflicts are not always political, ethnic, or religious in their orientation, nor are they evident only in armed clashes, revolts, or war but also in the contests, competitions, disputes, and tensions that characterize everyday life (1959); they can include explicit (overt) as well as latent (covert) events, to follow Parsons' terminology (1954:329). For all of these variations, conflict is present when there is an environment of human insecurity, or such an environment is imminent where conflict is present. Conflicts are likely to motivate people to move toward places where they perceive that the ongoing or potential conflict is relatively low or nonexistent. Thus, transnational moves often reflect conflictive situations in home communities or nations; blending the concept of transnationalism with conflict helps to avoid dichotomous categories of migrants and refugees, economic versus political migrants, and so on (Massey et al. 1998).

All migrations are culturally framed and socially defined by the migrants and nonmigrants and the conflicts and contests they are involved in and that they perceive. In other words, there is a cultural framework, or a culture of migration, that helps migrants define their mobility in relation to their household, home community, and world. A culture of migration relates to the strengths and weaknesses of the individual migrants themselves as well as the strengths and weaknesses of their homes, families, and sending and receiving communities, the sending and receiving nations, and the global patterns of social and economic life. A migrant's strengths and weaknesses reflect the gender, age, experience (including the experience in migration), schooling, and security and, the history and experiences of other movers and nonmovers involved in the social networks that characterize migration history and experience (and see Singer and Massey 1998).[7]

Early movers from countries with low rates of out-migration follow trajectories of a type that is quite different from those of migrants who leave countries with high rates of expulsion and rich histories of movement. The situation in Mexico illustrates this process clearly. For more than a century, Mexicans have moved to the U.S. from the country's central states, including Zacatecas, Durango, Jalisco, and Guanajuato.

On the other hand, a migrant from a "new" sending region—that is, a region without a tradition of migration and a history of movement, like the state of Chiapas—may lack a support network, needing to build one on his or her own (Téllez 2008; Villafuerte Solís and García Aguilar 2008). The linkages and experiences that ease the stresses and strains of border crossing, settlement, and job seeking are not present for the new mover. However, improved communication technologies such as the Internet and satellite television are making knowledge available across the globe (Chapman 2004). Today border crossings are not the unknown they were for those who crossed the Atlantic for new pastures at the turn of the last century. Yet the stories, motivations, and outcomes are often shared.

Understanding the culture of migration is critical as we work to define the motivations, outcomes, and possibilities that exist for movers and that encourage mobility. Migration can follow an internal path and take the migrant from her or his rural home to an urban setting. This pattern of movement is generally freer of federal intervention than is the crossing of international borders. However, moves can remain difficult as the migrant must deal with internal bigotries and internal socioeconomic problems that may arise as he or she moves (think of the Uighurs, who move from ethnic enclaves in rural western China to eastern cities and industrial centers). These stresses can be quite painful when they involve crossing ethnic or religious borders. On the other hand, migration to an international destination (which by definition must include crossing borders) typically places migrants at risk of capture, persecution, and perhaps jail time (this is particularly true for undocumented movers).

Life in a foreign country can be difficult even when the migrant is successful, finds work, earns a living, and remits to a hometown. Not surprisingly, many nonmigrants that Sirkeci and Cohen have encountered do not want to trade their lives in their communities of origin for the risks of life in a foreign country. Often the question "Why aren't there more migrants leaving?" is of more interest than "How many migrants are there?" As one Oaxacan farmer said when asked why he hadn't considered migrating to the U.S., "It isn't worth it! I'll earn a lot, but look at how much I have to spend, maybe $5,000! This just doesn't make sense; it isn't worth it for me. I'd rather stay here [Oaxaca, Mexico]" (interviewed May 2001). Similar sentiments were found among Turkish Kurdish immigrants in Cologne, Germany. Some felt that they had failed to achieve what they had intended, but they were unable to return to Turkey as they were too proud to admit failure. Put another way, they would not migrate if they were to begin again, yet, having migrated and failed, there was no way to return home (Sirkeci 2006a).

Nevertheless, the risks of international migration often do not outweigh the benefits, which can include higher wages, work and schooling opportunities, and security (Heyman 2007). This is the case even where home culture, language, and tradition are not shared with the majority of the community the migrant enters. There are also people who move as refugees and asylum seekers, such as contemporary Somalis, and for these individuals migration follows a path that may include years of living in camps and waiting for papers to be approved (Valentine, Sporton, and Nielsen 2009). Typically, once in a destination the refugee and asylum seeker is in a position quite different from that of the migrant and particularly the undocumented migrant (Zetter 2007). Refugee camps in Kenya, for example, limit the ability of Somalis to earn a living as they deny access and legally block active engagement with the larger national economy. Thus, Somalis not only must respond to the crises that put them in the camps in the first place, but they must also organize themselves to survive, to seek permanent settlement in new locales, and to maintain a sense of identity and social belonging (Kapteijns and Ali 2001). In a very different case, El Salvadorian immigrants who once held refugee status in the U.S. have seen that status shift as warfare and conflict in their sending country has declined. Now, one-time refugees must struggle against a system that recognizes them as extralegal immigrants. El Salvadorians in the U.S. face the new limits on their rights and potential deportation that come with their revised status (Coutin 2007).

To put all of this somewhat more succinctly: we have replaced the traditional view of migration—with its focus on movement from point A to point B for at least twelve months—with an emphasis on the culture of migration. The culture of migration identifies the abilities, limits, and needs of the mover as well as, importantly, the cultural traditions and social practices that frame those abilities and limitations through time. Finally, we note the national/international and transnational processes that render movement sensible, practical, and reasonable while also taking into account the enforcing factors.

While migration might look chaotic from afar, it is not a chaotic process. In fact, if migration was chaotic, people would not succeed as movers and mobility would hold little value. Therefore, we argue that migration makes sense and that it makes sense as a cultural process, an economic move, and a social event. Movers plan their sojourns and base their choices to migrate on real and perceived needs and benefits. Whether or not they see their plans through to their logical ends does not indicate that migration is chaotic or that mobility is a foolish choice. Rather, the outcomes of moving, regardless of the conclusions, are executed strategically and in a rational fashion. In other words, when a migrant leaves his or her home, he or she does so with a plan and a goal in mind. Even the moves of refugees who flee cultural, economic, religious, and social problems and persecution in their home communities and nations are typically making calculated decisions about their futures.

There are migrants who do not plan their sojourns, have no goals, and simply want to leave, must escape, or cannot stay. However, these migrants tend to form a small percentage of any group of movers. People do not typically pick up and move without forethought and some planning. We argue that even migrants who are described as "disappeared" are likely to have followed a clear plan of action in their decisions to leave. We base this belief on the fact that migration is a costly decision. Migrants who "disappear" (according to those family members or friends who are left behind) often have chosen to leave problematic and difficult relationships. Thus their decision was not random, but was in fact planned after consideration of the costs of remaining in a dysfunctional social arrangement (Ley and Kobayashi 2005; Osella and Osella 2000; Velayutham and Wise 2005).[8]

It is also critical to recognize and understand why people stay behind and do not migrate (Cohen 2002; Conway and Potter 2007; Faist 2000b; Fischer, Martin, and Staubhaar 1997).[9] A driving force for migrants is a combination of their needs and the needs and wants of those who cannot or will not migrate. To make sense of and organize their decisions, movers and nonmovers depend upon systems of cultural meaning framed in social processes. Coping with migration, contesting outcomes, challenging decisions, responding, and representing the future—all are part of what migrants and nonmigrants do as they negotiate movement. It is important to recognize the links with nonmovers in any migration decisions.

In the popular media, the migrant is often portrayed as a threatening individual or from a threatening group, someone who we as citizens of sovereign nations must fear and avoid. Migrants invade our lands and communities; they take our jobs and burden our schools and healthcare systems. Migrants drain away resources from natives who are most in need of those very benefits. Furthermore, there is an assumption that migrants often turn their backs on two systems—the one which they have left (their community and country of origin) and the one to which they have come (their community and nation of destination); and thus must be considered part of the insecurity factors for some others, as formulated in our conflict model (Sirkeci 2009).

In this book we argue that migrants are social actors making decisions about their futures that are framed by traditional beliefs, cultural expectations, and social practices and embedded in their immediate and broader environment, which is characterized by a variety of conflicts and competitions affecting the likelihoods of decisions to migrate. Thus we define migration as a rational and rationalizing act. It is not a decision made lightly, but rather a decision with far-reaching impacts (see Conway and Cohen 1998). This process of decision making and planning often takes a long time and may involve family members, relatives, and friends. It is a complicated, multifaceted, and often emotional decision.

It is wrong to assume that the migrants who have made it to the U.S. or Western Europe, among other places, are there for strictly economic or political reasons and are by definition a threat. As we will show, while migrants may share many motivations, they are not automatons and few are moving to join criminal groups or participate in illegal activities. Furthermore, shared motivations do not mean that outcomes will always be the same. To be more precise—while the pull of relatively high wages in destinations is a strong motivator to move, people migrate for many and multiple reasons while many others do not move at all. Movers often consider a variety of indicators to come up with the overall assessment of human insecurity and security that informs their decision to move. This consideration is not necessarily a systematic and accurate one but is largely shaped by individual circumstances and perceptions.

Consider young women who migrate from rural hometowns in Mexico or Turkey to escape abusive relationships at home. Other women cross to the U.S. and Europe to support their fathers and brothers who are established in destination communities. These young women often leave care-taking jobs in rural homes for the same sorts of positions in the U.S. and Europe, replacing the children and siblings they cared for at home with their working fathers and brothers. On the one hand, these women are caretakers for their relatives; on the other hand, they work to supplement family budgets and support children in their homes of origin. Not surprisingly, there are a growing number of women who migrate to seek out new opportunities independently. They also leave to join husbands who are established in destinations and reunify their families.[10] Nevertheless, these moves are also about security and reveal how people move from an environment of insecurity to relative security. These women arriving in destination countries may have bettered their lives compared to their fellow citizens who stay behind but are unlikely to enjoy the same level of security as their host-society members (for examples see Cuban 2009; Nadeau 2007; Thapar-Björkert 2007).[11]

A second example of the degree to which migration outcomes are related to such factors as cultural norms, social practices, and history comes from Sirkeci's work with Iraqis. Economic motives, while important in Iraq and among Iraqi migrants, are often superseded by the urge to find a secure and safe environment for self and family. Sirkeci (2006b) found that many Iraqis base much of their decision to migrate around the increasing sense that terrorism and insecurity are now part of life in places like Baghdad and that the only clear solution—that is, the only way to find a secure home—is to leave the homeland. There are hundreds of thousands of Iraqis struggling to leave their country—and while many of them seek work and opportunities where they can, nearly all seek simply to escape the violence and insecurity in Iraq. Sirkeci captured a detailed picture of such an exodus from an environment of human insecurity while studying Kurdish migration from Turkey, Turkmen emigration from Iraq in the 1990s and 2000s, and Lebanese flight after Israeli attacks in 2007 (Sirkeci 2005, 2006a, 2006b).

A third example comes from families that send their children to internal destinations in an effort to, first, enhance the socioeconomic status of a family in the place of origin through remittances and, second, reduce the burden a family places on local resources—an old migration model, to be sure, but also one that can affect and promote later transnational mobility. In sub-Saharan African countries like Zambia we find just such a process at work. Young men often leave their rural homes for the country's capital. These men can find it difficult to earn a living in their communities of origin and move not only for wages, but to ease pressures on sending house-holds, effectively reducing the number of individuals that a household's members must support in the moment (Cliggett 2000, 2003).

Perhaps more important for the discussion of global patterns of move-ment, there are also migrants who regularly return to their homes of ori-gin. These transmigrants travel between sending and receiving communi-ties following complex paths that link them to compatriots at many points (Levitt 2001). What these migrants bring home can be as important as the destinations to which they travel (Eder, Yakovlev, and Garkoglu 2003; Konstantinov 1996; Yukseker 2007).[12]

In many settings (including India, Turkey, Mexico, and El Salvador) the financial remittances returned by international migrants are critical to na-tional budgets as well as to homes and sending communities. In El Salva-dor, financial remittances are the largest source of income for the nation. In Brazil, migrants are celebrated as "national heroes" and the remittances that flow through the nation's banks are taxed by the state (Cohen 2005). Similarly, Lebanon is among the top recipients in terms of remittances per capita, constituting a significant share of the nation's wealth (Amery 1992).

The point of these examples is not that we must pick one variable and use it to explain outcomes (here economics, there politics; here labor mar-kets, there security), or even that we must measure all migrants equally, given their situations. Rather our point is that we need a model that allows us to define migration outcomes in relation to a variety of possibilities and in which we are not lost in the pursuit of numbers.

Understanding that about 200 million people are moving about the global landscape is a starting point and one through which we can under-stand national, macro-level trends, while a focus on the migrant typically emphasizes the impacts of movement on the individual, with less inter-est in larger patterns. But what if we look instead for a middle ground? A place where we can explore macro-trends, trends that often frame de-cision making at the national level with decision making at the personal level—in other words, the wants, desires, and limits that face households and their members around the world. This approach allows us to explore the economics behind migration decision making, without overlooking the cultural, political, and social decisions that migrants also make. While we reflect on what a migrant wants, we also keep track of the cultural and social boundaries that frame those wants and needs and the histories that limit making those decisions locally and prime a population to turn to migration.

Our goal through the remainder of this book is to develop a model of migration as a cultural process. To develop a cultural model of migration we build upon important work in anthropology, economics, geography, history, political science, psychology, and sociology. We believe that this approach is critical, as it emphasizes the dynamics of a culture of migration (not the decisions of individual migrants—what is best thought of as a micro-level approach—nor a focus on national outcomes—a macro-level analysis). We attempt to understand migration—or, better put, mobility—from the perspective of cultural and social practices while acknowledging national patterns and personal, micro-level differences.

The social universe (or meso-level) is where the decisions of individuals meet, where social practices and cultural beliefs engage, and where community traditions connect with personal and family choices. Because it builds upon work in migration studies, we believe that our book offers a new model and new "reading" of migration in the twenty-first century, one that should help advance the debate.

We have organized our work around particular themes and topics. We begin, not surprisingly, with the household. Our goal in the next chapter is to define the central importance of the household to migration outcomes. Using examples from throughout the world, we note how the very concept of the household has changed over time, as has the role that a household's members play in decision making. It is critical to realize that regardless of the moves a migrant makes (whether international or local, circular or one way), the decisions are framed within a larger social field than the individual—and for us that is the household. Even for the migrant who elects to leave a home and turn her or his back on a family, the decision to move will have repercussions that change the social universe for the household and those left behind. Furthermore, the developmental process that takes the household from founding to demise, or from its establishment at a marriage to its demise in death of its members, is critical to understanding migration decisions and outcomes. A young couple with small children from Bangladesh who sends a migrant to England to work in the service sector and send money home likely has a different set of needs and expectations then the older couple with grown children who are no longer at home. For this older couple, remittances are not hoarded to educate children; rather, remittances can be invested in new and different ways and create a different set of opportunities.

We follow our discussion of the household with an exploration of contemporary migration. While we focus generally on the last several decades of movement and the importance that local and global patterns play in driving contemporary movement, it also remains critical to understand the historical underpinnings of migration. Furthermore, it is vital to place international migration and transmigration into a discussion that recognizes the continued value of internal moves, refugee movement, and the lives of asylum seekers.

The next two chapters look specifically at internal and international movers. Our goal in these chapters is to show first that we cannot fully understand migration patterns if we ignore internal moves. Often these migrations are the first step a sojourner makes as he or she embarks on more involved border crossings. For other migrants, internal moves fulfill the basic needs and demands of the household and thus there is no further movement. It is also critical to understand that internal movement can be motivated by factors that are quite different from those that influence international movers; we thus use several different examples to show the wealth of meaning associated with internal moves. As we progress to international movers, we focus again on the role culture and households play in decision making. We use examples from around the world to explore the local meanings of migration and the impacts of economics, work, etc., on movers and nonmovers. It is important to underline again that the link between international and internal migrations is not a one-way street. Movers may follow a step process, as they move from an internal to an international destination, yet this is not a fixed rule.

In Chapter 5 we consider nonmovers, those individuals who stay at home even as migrants leave. Oftentimes it is easy to ignore stay-at-homes and nonmovers in the discussion of migration; even in discussions of the role households play, nonmovers are seen as fairly passive decision makers. The real decision makers, or at least those actively involved in decision making, are the migrants. In this chapter we will also expand upon the idea of mobility and move away from the notion of a linear, yearlong migration to capture the full picture of international mobility, which is much broader than the U.N. definition allows.

Chapter 6 focuses on the economic impacts of migration. It is not difficult to recognize the overwhelming role that financial remittances play in the health and well-being of migrant-sending countries (like Mexico, El Salvador, and Lebanon, for example); nevertheless, money is not shared equally, and people remit material as well as financial resources. In this chapter we look specifically at the impacts that various kinds of remittances have on sending households and communities and we disaggregate national data that give us the overall impact of remittances to show what individuals do. However, our discussion is not limited to remittances. Immigrants' contributions to their host economies need to be acknowledged too. Therefore we will also discuss the gains from immigration.

To further frame our work and to clearly outline our interests we review key issues in migration studies and the theories that have developed through time and from various fields. We develop a concise set of terms and definitions to help the reader follow our discussion and to effectively meet and critique our model. Our goal is not to limit the debate on migration, but to bring better precision to that debate in an effort to move away from unidimensional models.

Our goal in this book is to illuminate the lives and experiences of the people behind the numbers and to inform you, the reader, about why it is important to look beyond these raw totals. We argue that it is critical to move away from caricatures of migrants as lonely individuals without homes, dangerous rogues out to take jobs from unsuspecting citizens, and poor people avoiding responsibility and seeking employment and financial enrichment at the expense of their families, sending communities, and home nations. Such depictions are promulgated by tabloid media and chauvinist groups. Many governments may need to see figures such as the ones provided by the U.N. for planning and policy purposes; however, there is strong evidence that migration includes more than those individuals who stay for at least a year, as well as others who move more often.

Of course, all of those movers, short and long term, internal and international, have needs and wants. Their decisions have a bearing on settled populations, populations left behind, and populations at their destination. All of these groups have demands and they must be provided for. Perhaps we can approach mobility and migration using a basic marketing definition—a definition that assumes individuals have nearly limitless needs and wants but only limited means through which to satisfy them. In this situation migration becomes an important avenue toward satisfying those wants—not all of them, but certainly more than might be possible without migration. Mobility is not a perfect answer for the individual as he or she remains with certain wants and needs that can never be fully met. In other words, mobility is not a panacea. Nevertheless, it is a fairly complex response to needs and wants and often allows for the individual mover to secure at least some of the needs he or she has defined.

One   THE HOUSEHOLD IN A
GLOBAL PERSPECTIVE

*I think her being there [abroad] is good for me because she
helps me. If she was here maybe she could help in different ways,
however for me it is important that she is there since I get money
to pay for school. . . . So the benefit of my mom being in the U.S.
is economic. We always have food and my grandmother doesn't
worry as much as she did before about money.*
— GUILLERMO, THE SON OF A HONDURAN
TRANSNATIONAL MIGRANT WORKING IN THE U.S.

*The Filipino family has become transnational in an effort to
protect itself from declining real incomes and standards of living,
and to achieve family aims for investment in education and
acquisition of other productive assets including land and housing.*
— ABELLA, 1993

Many researchers focus on migrants and the decisions that
drive their mobility and the outcomes of their moves. Of course, the decision to migrate is in the hands of the mover. Nevertheless, it is a mistake to think of the migrant as a lone decision maker, just as it is a mistake
to think of the migrant in her or his destination community as a rogue
individual. The decision to migrate, while in the hands of the individual
mover, is made in reference to and relation with many other actors and includes other people, places, processes, promises, and potential outcomes.
In this chapter we explore how the decision to migrate is made and look
beyond the individual.

The decision to migrate takes place in reference to the strengths and
weaknesses of the mover, but also in reference to the strengths and weaknesses of her or his household. Beyond the household, the community,
sending nation, and receiving country influence outcomes. Economic and

social patterns link origin and destination communities and include the pulls and pushes of wage and labor markets, immigration policies, cultural values, and traditions, and macro-level socioeconomic processes. The key decision-making structure is the household, where all (or at least most) of the factors influencing outcomes come together.

A focus on the household may seem counterintuitive, particularly given the power of the global labor market, and the pull of relatively high wages, to drive migration patterns. Yet consider this: even the migrant who denies his family, abandons her household, and forsakes a community to find a job in a foreign land is making a decision that is in response to the strengths and weaknesses of her or his specific household. In this respect, the Georgian woman who flees her household and hometown to organize a new life around a new job and opportunities in a new setting is making a household decision. For the people she leaves behind, the outcome of her decision to migrate can be devastating (Buckley 1997). The origin household is left with one less engaged member and the loss is apparent for all to see. Certainly, migration is a very difficult decision with far-reaching impacts. It is not that different for the Nicaraguan household whose son leaves for the promise of work in a Mexico City store. The promise of work in Mexico City and the income the job will provide likely will do little to enhance the status of the Nicaraguan sending household. The young man's decision is made in reference to a dream and a possibility, and even though he may consult family and friends, his decision could impoverish his sending household. Nevertheless, once the decision is made it creates a series of new concerns for the household and its members as to how they will deal with the loss.

What we hope is apparent from these brief examples are the processes and boundaries that define the household structure of decision making (see fig. 1.1). The individual mover (like his or her nonmoving relatives and friends) is embedded in the household, and her or his migration decisions reflect broader external forces that are defined by the individual but also by the community, region, state, nation, and global process (Pennartz and Niehof 1999).

THE MIGRANT'S DECISION

Migration is a complex decision and it does not happen suddenly. Individuals in Mexico do not wake up and think, *Today I will go to the U.S.*, nor do Pakistanis arise one morning and decide, *Okay, it is time to leave*

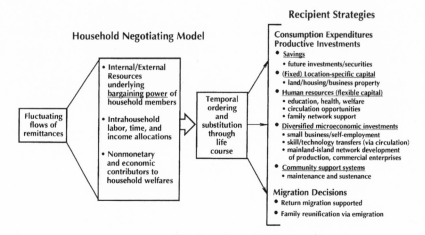

FIGURE 1.1.   *Modeling household migration (from Conway and Cohen 1998:30).*

for London. As a complex decision, the choice to migrate is influenced by many factors; some factors are defined by the individual, and others by the individual's household and community. Finally, there are external forces that frame migration outcomes and that develop from global economic and social patterns and processes.

The potential mover has much to consider as he or she ponders the value of migration. His age and her marital status are both critical to outcomes. Gender can open or potentially close doors to certain moves. Education and experience are also critical to the success of a migrant, as are her or his wealth and skills. No one factor will determine the outcome of the decision to move, or of migration. Of course the decision lies with the individual (regardless of the factors that influence it) and may not correspond to the social scientist's expectations for life.[1]

An individual's age, marital status, and gender are perhaps the most basic determinants in migration decision making and outcomes. Young movers follow paths that are unique, the newly married make choices that are different from those of unmarried movers, and women make decisions that are often fundamentally different from those of men. A migrant's age is a critical factor. The moves of young men and women—men and women who are not adult (and adulthood is often culturally defined)—are circumscribed by the rules and social regulations defined by parents and elders. Younger movers typically frame their sojourns in terms of the needs and desires of their families. Parents send their children to jobs and opportunities away from home and often with little input from the child him- or herself. This is particularly true when the child is, in effect, sold to an outsider who will employ him or her—perhaps in the sex trade, as is too often the fate of young girls in Thailand and Burma (Kempadoo and Doezema 1998; Kitiarsa 2008; Quirk 2007). Children also benefit from the decisions of their parents, and they may find themselves enrolled in school programs that demand they leave their natal homes. Such moves are often premised on the assumption that the child will support her or his family once a skill is mastered. This is the case among Filipinos who will go into debt to send their children to training programs at national universities, where they can master new skills as nurses and caregivers. Parents assume their children will take their newfound skills, gain employment in the U.S., and support their families in the Philippines once they have established themselves in North America (Kingma 2005; Parreñas 2005).

Thousands of students migrate to gain access to universities and for the jobs and incomes that higher education brings (Zhao 1999). The selection and admission processes in each country impose a set of particular expectations for young movers. Nevertheless many young people make their first long-term moves when they enroll for a university degree. Here again gendered attitudes may determine the patterns, disadvantaging girls in some countries.[2] Those in developing or less-developed countries face a bigger challenge in the search for higher education. Often they have to move to another country to escape bigotries and cultural limitations and to access strong, recognized programs, particularly for postgraduate studies.

Older children can sometimes ignore the demands of their parents. Once a child is in her or his late teens he or she is better able to make decisions and can exercise a degree of self-determination. The costs of migration are still likely to be covered by a family or family friends and there may be some demands placed on the young mover, yet often the mover is able to define a path that begins to establish some independence.

Once settled, young movers, particularly young men, are often seen as a threat by members of a destination country. For instance, North Americans often assume that nearly any young, male Latino immigrant to the U.S. is a member of a gang, involved in smuggling drugs, or interested in escaping his past rather than supporting a sending household. The same basic problem confronts young Muslim, Middle Eastern, and North African immigrants to Europe. To the French, German, and British, among others, these young men are terrorists or criminal threats and pose real danger to the young women it is assumed that they target.[3]

It is quite often the case that the young (male) members of the family go abroad and, once settled, try to help and enable others to join them. This is relevant to conflict cases, where human insecurity is strong, as with Turkish Kurds in the 1990s and early 2000s. Turkish Kurds migrated to Germany not simply for work, but also to escape persecution at home. And while they encountered new kinds of discrimination in Germany, it was not motivated by the anti-Kurdish trends present within Turkey. Many young Kurds arrived in Europe in search of a sense of security, and once established, they waited to be joined by brothers, sisters, and parents. The young son's or brother's migration is thus part of a household strategy used to overcome the environment of human insecurity felt in the origin community.

The challenges that young movers face in their destinations can confront them at home as well. Young movers might be mistrusted by their families and their sending communities. If they decide to migrate with little support from their natal, sending homes, there arises the sentiment that they are escaping or fleeing responsibilities. They often leave work that although poorly paid, nevertheless contributes to cover the daily costs of living in a direct and immediate way, replacing one set of costs and benefits with a different but sometimes no less problematic set.

The sending household does not wait for remittances that may never materialize; rather it creates new strategies to deal with the loss. Finally, there is often the sense that a young mover who leaves without the direct intervention of her or his family has turned away from the sending household and severed any relationship with her or his family. While this may be true, often the young migrant who leaves maintains some connections over time, and even if these connections are not strong, they can become the basis for links that reemerge at a later date. These renewed links usually emerge as the settled migrant and her or his success allow for engagement with sending households and origin communities.

Marital status is a second variable that influences migration outcomes. Young, unmarried migrants make decisions that are fundamentally different from those of a newly married or a well-established couple. Young, unmarried migrants move for their natal families and for themselves. Married migrants move for their own families and young children: to cover the costs of weddings, homebuilding, and improvements as well as educational expenses. Schmalzbauer (2008) provides us rich examples from among Honduran families. Nineteen-year-old Guillermo (quoted earlier), like many other Hondurans, benefits from family migration—his parents earn money in the U.S. to finance his education in a Honduran university, which will better his employment chances:

> "With a high school degree one can't earn much, only 70–80 percent (of a good salary). With a university degree one can get 90–100 percent. . . . My idea is to continue with international marketing [studies] and then if possible I would like to get a masters degree in finance. . . . After finishing school what I want the most is to open my own business. . . . I am very positive." (Schmalzbauer 2008:340)

Older couples with older children and couples who are established in their households and communities face a different set of decisions when thinking about mobility. Now that the costs of a child's education may be a nonfactor for the couple, they can use their remittances for home improvements. The older migrant is likely moving to accomplish one of several goals (whether realistic or not). He or she may wish to begin to organize the capital needed to invest or expand a local business and in a small way support a community's social reproduction and maintenance (Boehm 2008; Dreby 2006; Hondagneu-Sotelo 1994; Oropesa and Landale 1997; Voigt-Graf 2008). Alternatively, an older mover might travel as a tourist to visit family already settled elsewhere and in the process organize resources to resettle in the future.

Gender impacts outcomes and married men and women make different decisions. Married men typically use their families as a reason to migrate. They make the sojourns they do to earn the money necessary to cover the costs of education, health, weddings, and so on. Thus, a Chinese illegal migrant apprehended in Belgium says:

> I am the only breadwinner in the family. I am responsible for my wife, my son and my old mother. My father has passed away. I earn 300 Yuan per month in my village. This is not much. With this amount I cannot support my family. My son stopped going to school because we don't have money. My wife is sick. (Pang 2007:99)

Married women often face a series of traditional beliefs that are barriers to mobility and suggest their migrations are problematic at best and extremely dangerous at worse. In transnational migration, they are likely to follow the trajectories of their spouses, brothers, or fathers and often with a certain time lag. Their resources also go to the family, but where men can have an adventure, women are at risk. And it is only in recent years that migrant women have begun to work independently and for themselves rather than for their families (Donato et al. 2006; INSTRAW 2007; Nolin 2006).

It is obvious that men and women follow different paths as migrants; they often travel to different destinations and for different reasons and once settled they access different jobs. Yet gender also influences outcomes before migration takes place. Men and women encounter different barriers to decision making at home as well as abroad. Gender impacts migration outcomes from a young age as rural women and women who are members of families living in poverty are removed from schools at a younger age and often before the boys around them. Furthermore, younger women, when they are encouraged to continue their education, are channeled into traditionally female careers, which can also narrow options for new migrants. Transnational mobility frequently places these young women in jobs for which they are overqualified. Careers as domestic workers are one good example. A recent U.K. study showed that women's qualifications and skills are often ignored by their clients and they are forced into a career path with no upward mobility (Cuban 2009).

While young men may have the ability to migrate nearly anywhere within reason—particularly if they are not married—young women typically find their destination choices circumscribed by family, community, and traditional concepts of correct gendered behavior.[4] In many settings young men are expected to migrate. They move as a "rite of passage," a signal that they are adults and can care for themselves. Women, on the other hand, are not so free to travel and often their travels are not deemed as valuable. This is partly due to traditions in sending societies but is also the result of restrictions imposed by receiving countries. While Arab countries, for instance, remain a major destination for female movers from southeast Asia (a group that is mainly employed as domestic workers), Turkish migration to Arab countries was almost completely male-dominated and focused on construction (Icduygu and Sirkeci 1998).[5]

Young women in southern Mexico find that there are many barriers to crossing the U.S. border.[6] Even before they consider the dangers of the borderlands and the challenges of U.S. immigration laws, traditional local practices in sending households can severely limit the opportunities open to women. Cerrutti and Massey argue that "in Mexico, who migrates and why is likely to be related strongly to gender and household position"

(2001:190), and the pattern would seem to apply elsewhere as well (see also Curran et al. 2006). In fact, in southern Mexico the assumption is that women should stay home. It is only in their homes that women are safe and not threatened. Young women who travel across the border face many challenges, including becoming a crime statistic, getting involved in the sex trade, and being abused. The fear, however, is likely not so much that women will be victimized once across the border as that the families sending these women will lose control of them and their earnings.

In response to the pressures not to travel across an international border, young women are encouraged, if they want to migrate, to move to an internal destination. For example, "women from the Philippines show higher rates of rural–urban migration than men; moreover, Filipinas are more likely than men to migrate as teenagers, well before marriage" (Lauby and Stark 1987:1; Nadeau 2007).[7] Nevertheless, when young women do manage to migrate to the U.S., they often travel as daughters and sisters; once they are settled in the U.S., they often find that they must care for their families and the time they have available for work is limited by the demands that their new households place on them. A striking example of gender selectivity imposed by government policies is found in Portugal, where the government issued passports only to men until 1989 (Brettell 1995). Women and children were supposed to travel on men's passports as dependents. Even after the policy changed Portuguese women had to seek permission from their husbands to travel abroad.

While Latina women are encouraged to stay close to home, in other situations women are encouraged to travel to foreign destinations. For instance, women are also recruited to particular jobs, such as domestic care or nursing (Cuban 2009; Nadeau 2007; Pojmann 2007). Chinese rural-to-urban migration is often focused on young women, who fill factory jobs in part because of the assumption that they are better at the repetitive kinds of labor that is available (Myerson et al. 2010). Of course, the fact that these women are paid less than men for their work further increases their attractiveness to employers (He and Gober 2003).

Gender also has a bearing on remittance practices by migrants. Immigrant men typically find better-paying jobs than do women even though they are paid less than the nonmovers in the host community. Additionally, women find that they assume caretaker roles in their new communities and often must balance this demand against the requirements of work. Men may also have time to find a second job and earn additional income. It is often the case that because women continually remit, or remit more consistently over time, they return more money to their homes than their male compatriots over the long run (Fomby 2005; Gamburd 2008; Georges 1992; Wong 2006). Nevertheless, while women do tend to remit over longer periods and more regularly than do men, over the short term men remit more than do women.

HOUSEHOLDS AND MIGRATION

Just as no two migrants are equal but instead reflect special skills, age, abilities, and values, so too are the households that migrants come from unique. Migrant households bring strengths and weaknesses to the decision processes. For our purposes, a household is more than the building within which a family or domestic group lives. The building is a home—nothing more than a structure—and it is dangerous to assume that the physical structure is the household or that the people who matter in decision making are the individuals who live in that structure at a particular moment in time (Guyer 1981; Wilk 1989).

The household's structure may indicate some social realities and symbolically represent and create identity; nevertheless, the relationship of the household to its meaning is not direct nor should it be assumed to be unproblematic (Netting, Wilk, and Arnauld 1984). Furthermore, we should not assume that the household's structure has been determined solely by systems of production and demographic processes (Goody 1972). Such a perspective misses the creative, active, and adaptive ways in which the household is formed and through which it forms and informs social process (Netting, Wilk, and Arnauld 1984; Wilk 1991). Thus, we argue that the household is created by, around, and in reference to the people who live in it. It reflects history, but is not historic; it gives physical definition to a domestic unit, a group of people (sometimes but not always a family and not always a family that is easily recognized), but it also transcends place to include individuals (like migrants) who live in a variety of places and destinations.

Households reflect and build upon the history and the cultural ideals and social norms of the people who create them (Netting, Wilk, and Arnauld 1984). While some households develop around a nuclear family unit (the typical Western household of a married couple and children), others reflect a very different logic. We might encounter extended families (multigenerational units within a broad set of kin members living together), blended households that include members from a variety of formally and informally linked units, or single parent–headed households. The common thread that links households is their purpose and role, not their defined structure or their determined organization, for these can be quite fluid. Garifuna households in Belize are an example of what we mean. The Garifuna, an Afro-Caribbean society living on the coast of Belize, organize their families and households along regularly changing patterns. Most households are female-headed and visited by a series of men who share responsibilities for the children they have sired. The men, who earn their money through work on fishing boats and international migration to the U.S., intermittently invest in the women and children with whom they are involved. They show up from time to time and lavish gifts on the women they co-habitate with and their children. Thus, for the Garifuna the household is a fluid unit whose membership changes over time and expands to include men when they are present, but contracts as well when those men leave; and through every change social authority and power is held by women and passed down through generations (González 1988).

The example of the Garifuna reminds us that what identifies a household is the role it plays in the social lives of its members. Households are "dynamic and changeable" (Wilk 1991:39). They are also contradictory in that the very structures that create the household (and that the household creates in return) are linked to social, economic, natural, and historical processes that are always changing and sometimes conflictive (Taylor et al. 2005). In other words, even as authority is being organized within the household, that authority may change, leadership can be replaced and reorganized, and membership can be restructured. Such a pattern is evident in Somali refugee households, where women increasingly organize and support households that are traditionally patrilineal and structured around male-centered social hierarchies. Somali women, who find jobs more easily in the diaspora, are more and more heading households as single mothers. Their allegiance lies with their mothers and fathers and the patrilines they were born into, not those that define their spouses. In an interesting twist, Somali women preserve and reconstruct traditional society in the diaspora around a core of linked female-dominated households that establish new relationships even as a traditional identity is created around Islam and Koranic law (Al-Sharmani 2006; Fuglerud and Engebrigtsen 2006).

Households are also finite units. They have a beginning and an end, they exist in specific places and over time, and they have histories, trajectories, and meanings. Some of the earliest work in anthropology identified how the household develops—or, as put by Meyer Fortes, how the household follows a developmental cycle (1971). What Fortes meant is that the household's growth is not random; rather, it is established at the marriage of two individuals. Over time, the household expands as children are added. Responsibility also increases as young newlyweds become parents, as parents become important citizens, and as citizens assume authority positions in a community. The period of expansion is replaced by a trend toward consolidation as the children in the household grow to be adults and move out and on, often to establish their own new households. This point often marks the zenith of the household members' powers, as the time needed to care for children is now donated to the community at large. Finally, as the members of a household age, so too does the household itself, and it will finally collapse as its founders pass away.

The household also serves a symbolic and ideological purpose for its members and for the larger communities within which it exists. Households are settings where education takes place, where individuals learn about what is correct and incorrect, and what is morally important and culturally valued. Members thus learn social roles and the social rules they must follow. Our point is not that individuals simply fill household positions like automatons. Rather, it is within the households that sanctions on behavior, what is right and wrong, and the meaning and value of cultural beliefs are established, reproduced, and contested. The identities that are established can include that of the migrant. He or she fits into the broader system. The potential to migrate brings with it specific ideas of what a migrant should do. He or she should ideally support his or her sending household and invest in its well-being. A natal community should also find itself valued by the migrant.

The household as a social setting is not only a place where meaningful cultural beliefs are practiced. The household is also the setting where those practices are produced, recreated, and changed, as we noted in the examples of the Garifuna and Somali women. In other words, households do not merely reflect cultural values as if they were part of some kind of rote memory exercise; rather, the household is integral in the negotiation of meaning and is critical to the creation and maintenance of identity over time (Netting 1993).

The household does not create opportunities for migration—rather, opportunities grow from the abilities, strengths, and weaknesses of individuals and from the fixed and flexible resources that characterize the household (Conway 2000; Conway and Cohen 1998). Fixed resources (see fig. 1.1) include those items that are directly defined and linked to the household and tend not to change through time. Flexible resources are those things including wealth that define the household but shift over time and space. Thus, land is typically a fixed resource for most migrants. It is a source of wealth and, at least for some peoples (particularly in the past), a resource that is critical because it can be used productively. Other capital investments, including the physical home, businesses, animals, and large domestic goods are often fixed, although they tend to have specific starting points on the calendar.

Though they may change through time, households are fixed resources for most migrants. They are physically real and set in time and space. Households are also social resources, serving as a central node for their members and individuals (movers and nonmovers) who develop familial, kin-, and friend-based systems of support. In other words, a household is a symbolically fixed resource that serves as an anchor for the migrant and members. Wealth (both economic and social) can be fixed or flexible. A household's members can build upon wealth as they deploy it to support their decision. Wealth is also flexible, and one outcome of migration is the creation of wealth that can grow over time and be translated from flexible to fixed. In other words, as a migrant is successful, that success translates from perceived to real social status in a community. This is clear in the actions of migrants who hail from San Francisco Cajonos, Oaxaca, Mexico (Sanchez 2007). The town of San Francisco Cajonos has less than one hundred citizens living in it today, yet there are thousands of migrants who call San Francisco Cajonos home and who live in Oaxaca City (the state's capital), Mexico City (the nation's capital), and Los Angeles, California, one of the most important Oaxaqueño destinations in the U.S. San Franciscans who have emigrated and the children of those emigrants continue to return throughout the year to their hometown in Oaxaca's mountains, Sierra Madre Occidental (also called the Sierra de Juarez in honor of Benito Juarez, a national hero, president, and leader of the struggles for Mexican Independence from Spain, who is a native to the region). Every year, some San Franciscans return to their town to serve in the local political hierarchy. Their service in San Francisco builds social status and social capital that follows a traditional model of community organization that is present throughout rural Oaxaca (Hernández Díaz 2007).

Service "at home" translates to San Franciscan communities in Los Angeles as well. Thus, social status earned in San Francisco Cajonos, Oaxaca, is flexible in its organization (it can be used nearly anywhere) as long as people share social meaning and cultural values. In a general sense, status is flexible, in that it works regardless of community, but also fixed through support for the hometown that anchors identity and serves as a symbolic homeland (for comparison, see Paerregaard 2008).

Flexible resources are those things that contribute to a household's well-being over time, but can shift quite dramatically. Income and labor practices within a household are perhaps the most critical of flexible resources that a potential migrant can draw on as he or she makes a decision to move. So too are the temporary demands that a household places on its members, for instance, requiring that a member take on new responsibilities. The goods and services a household demands also change over time as new technologies and possibilities emerge. Finally, the very perceptions that characterize how a household's members approach important decisions can have a profound effect on outcomes. When migration is not a typical or common choice, the household may exercise control over decision making. On the other hand, as migration grows more common, a household's leaders may relax their pressure on family members to stay put and push internal mobility and international border crossing as important opportunities.

Households are constantly transforming themselves and being transformed as times change, people move and grow, and societies vary from stratum to stratum and over time. What we mean, then, is that households not only reflect the immediate needs, desires, and possibilities of their members, but also help to form those needs, desires, and possibilities. Households also reflect and form the very fabric of local society, for through households, citizens establish identities, create powerful and long-lasting associations, and, one hopes, thrive.[8]

Households are not created equal. Not only are there wealthy and poor households and high- and low-status households (although in relative terms), but households also develop over time and go through specific stages. Thus the young family, just starting out and with very young children, represents a kind of household that is different from that of the older family with grown children. When it comes to migration, these two families may follow similar paths and send members to a distant location for work, but the outcomes of those migrations and the uses of the remittances resulting from those migrations are likely to be quite different. The young family will use migration to enable them to cover the immediate expenses that come with raising young children. The older family may use the remittances from migration to open a small business. The point is that the household and the family that is based within it have a direct impact on the outcomes of migration.

BEYOND THE HOUSEHOLD:
THE ROLE OF COMMUNITY
IN MIGRATION DECISIONS

Migration decisions reach beyond the household to include communities, origin countries, and destinations. A decision to migrate thus reflects not only a household, but the interaction and integration of households, communities, countries, and the globe. It is critical to capture how households work together to maximize resources that will support decision making while minimizing the challenges that the individual may face. Households with migrants as members tend to work together. The linkages that tie a migrant to his or her household and hometown also create an important bond to other movers. In fact, a majority of movers follow such paths as they make their decisions and follow earlier movers who are often family or friends (Massey, Goldring, and Durand 1994). One of the signs of a mature migrant flow is that the very social ties that make migration possible become so common as to connect nearly every household to a migrant, although in many settings there remain nonmigrant or nonmover households. These households typically lack the bonds and relationships that will support easy movement.

Intra-household relationships are critical to decision making. Potential migrants learn from other households about the challenges they face as movers as well as the opportunities they will find once they reach their destination. The links with movers and their households also translate to important and positive ties that can be exploited to help cross a border. In other words, knowing a migrant means that the resources he or she has gained can help new movers as they cross borders, find smugglers, perhaps purchase papers, and move goods.

Social connections to earlier movers and their households are absolutely critical as the new migrant settles in his or her destination community and begins to search for work (Massey 1990). These connections are also important while the new migrant is entering a new set of relationships that bring with them their own unique challenges and opportunities. Central here is that the relationships the new mover holds with his household and with the households of other movers become a foundation upon which his social life is constructed—but a social life that is defined by the cultural beliefs and traditional practices of the origin community (Paerregaard 2008).

Differences and similarities between origin and destination countries also influence migration outcomes. Often these differences are defined around the push-and-pull factors that drive migrants from one country to another. The influences of labor markets, wages, and job opportunities are clear where migration is a rule. Movers leave to seek jobs when no or few opportunities are present in their home community. They are looking for relatively higher wages that typically dwarf the wages available in their origin country, and they seek opportunities to establish themselves in ways that are unavailable at home.

A focus on the economics of migration and the push-and-pull of labor markets can obscure other forces that influence migration decision making. There are migrants who seek destinations that will allow them to voice political opinions that may not be respected at home. Political figures who fled countries such as Burma, Thailand, and Iran can be counted among the many examples. Similarly, massive refugee flows from Turkey to Western Europe in the early 1980s in reaction to the military intervention of September 1980 constitute a good case. During the 1990s, Kurdish asylum seekers arrived in almost every industrialized democratic country to escape tensions and unrest in Turkey. Today these Kurdish migrants form strong and influential diasporic communities in Canada, Sweden, the U.K., Germany, the Netherlands, and France. Refugees and asylum seekers often have few choices in terms of their destinations, but are aiming to escape a sense of human insecurity and move toward relatively more secure places.

Finally, and while it may seem odd, there are the unique needs of leisure movers, highly educated movers, and the elderly, who are often looking for a relatively cheaper lifestyle that will maximize their retirement savings. While the retiree and tourist and highly educated movers are quite different from the migrants we have focused on, the patterns followed are similar and reflect household resources. Thus, we should not be surprised that we have seen a surge in the volume of Western European pensioners migrating to Hungary, where their limited pension incomes go further compared to that in their countries of origin (Illes 2005). These older migrants often join their sons and daughters, sometimes at their offsprings' request, because maintaining the family is cheaper for the younger generation as their parents join them in Hungary.

CONCLUSIONS

As our discussion suggests, while the decision to migrate is made by the individual and constructed around the household, it often isn't enough to think about a household as a single unit or to define the migrant as a person who exists in a single place. People belong to more than one household. We often establish households upon marriage and in adulthood; nevertheless, we remain (regardless of changing status and participation) members of our natal households and perhaps more.

In addition, households exist across space, and include individuals in different settings and different circumstances. Specifically, when we are interested in migration, we need to recognize the importance of "transnational households" and transnational communities. Transnational households and communities exist in two and sometimes more settings and can often bring together individuals as single domestic units and as inclusive social groups. In other words, in a transnational setting we often find that individual migrants remit to a specific household, supporting and maintaining that household or domestic group over time in a larger community that includes many households following a similar trajectory.

There are of course situations where the transnational household struggles, just as there are examples of people cooperating. Migrant and transnational households can be dysfunctional. Orozco notes that while he was working with household heads in Oaxaca, these individuals would often inform him that a child now residing in the U.S. had ceased to interact with their origin household (2002). Their remittances had stopped and they were no longer investing in the life of the town. Perhaps they had their own family in their new destination, perhaps they had gained new citizenship or lost a job, but for some reason the connections were broken. Nevertheless, what we typically find in migrant and transnational households are strong bonds between those members who stay behind and those members who establish themselves in new destinations.

The household is not a static unit; rather, it changes over time in terms of its needs, demands, and structure. Often we make the mistake of assuming that households are monolithic and unchanging. In fact, as households mature, demands change. Younger households often frame their wants, needs, and demands in terms of the immediate materials necessary to complete building a structure or to modernize their living space. The presence of children brings with it a second set of needs—cash is necessary to meet the desires of the children, but also to cover the costs of education and schooling.[9]

We use a household-based approach to understand how migration outcomes impact local social systems. Our approach contrasts with a focus on the individual on one hand and national level factors on the other and parallels what Faist (1997) refers to as the meso-level to understand broadly based patterns of movement. A household model also contrasts with a focus on the psychological motivations of the individual actor or decision maker. While the other two approaches have important strengths, neither adequately accounts for the social universe that defines migration for most global movers. Thus, our concept of the household as the center of decision making, and migration as a process that typically takes account of the household and its needs, is critical to understanding the economics and culture of migration.

Households are important linkages for migrants and the children of migrants who are new movers and for those who have settled in new communities. The ties to home give the migrant a sense of meaningful belonging and act as an anchor when a receiving community is less than supportive of the migrants who have arrived. The migrant is also linked to the household through important social bonds and cultural expectations. Whether correctly or not, often migration is framed as an activity that one undertakes in the name of a household. A common refrain throughout southern Mexico was that migration was a move made in the name of the family and household. It was something done to support others, a selfless act rooted in the reciprocal bonds that are created in the household and that link the members together.

Two

THE GROWTH OF MIGRATION

Mobility, Security, Insecurity

> *There is no room in this country for the man who tries to be*
> *both an American and something else. . . . Every immigrant*
> *who comes here should be required within five years to learn*
> *English or leave the country.*
> —THEODORE ROOSEVELT, 1918

EARLY MIGRATION MODELS

There was a time when immigration was assumed to fol-
low a direct and highly regular and regulated path from a place of origin
to a place of destination (see Ravenstein 1889). Migration was conceptual-
ized as a normal act, one that followed predictable laws with well-defined
outcomes and in which people, as movers, followed preset pathways. In
other words, migrants were assumed to move as new jobs and opportunities became available or as their social traditions might determine. For
the latter, you might think of the way anthropologists traditionally talked
about hunter-gatherers. Hunter-gatherers, because they rely upon forag-
ing for their livelihood, followed fairly set rounds, traveling from food
source to food source and water hole to water hole. This straightforward
approach to the definition of migration was powerful for researchers and
has had profound staying power. The United Nations' definition of migration (2006) owes more to Ravenstein's laws of migration than it does to the
contemporary realities of movers around the world. Despite the efforts of
qualitative researchers, feminists, and postmodernist scholars over several
decades, we are still trying to acknowledge that human migration is a process that can be rather complex.

To be fair, much of the early work on migration reflected what researchers found as they engaged the topic. Unlike anthropologists, ethno-

graphically leaning geographers, and sociologists, who were often concerned with social agency, early migration researchers did not look at how migrants behaved and were largely interested in the macro-level patterns involved in movement. Furthermore, many early researchers assumed that individuals followed the dictates of strong social structures (rules and regulations) and profound social roles (see writings on social organization by Emile Durkheim and social functionalism by A. R. Radcliffe Brown, among others, for examples from sociology and anthropology) that were rooted in timeless and complex cultural motivators (often called traditions). In such situations, there was little to no room for individuals to exercise their will and make choices and even less room for unanticipated consequences.

Given these strictures, early models of migration assumed migrants who embarked on sojourns left homes, hometowns, and nations destined for foreign shores and the chance to join a new country or better labor markets. Thus, those immigrants destined for the U.S. (80 percent of whom were northern and western Europeans prior to 1890 and who shifted to eastern, south, and central Europe by the early twentieth century) were described as coming to America to become citizens, to "enrich" the nation and, in the process, themselves. Gerstle describes this phase of U.S.-bound immigration as coercive and built around the effort to assimilate non-native citizens. "In schools, at workplaces, at settlement houses, and in politics, they taught immigrants English, the essentials of American citizenship, skills useful in getting decent employment, and faith in American values and institutions" (1999:277). One of the inherent problems for the migrant developed in some destination countries, as we will see below, as their communities grew to become more diverse and to challenge the core beliefs of the receiving culture. For example, immigrants to South America (Japanese immigrants to Peru and Europeans to Argentina) encountered intense xenophobia as their successes mounted and challenged local assumptions concerning authority and status (Masterson and Funada-Classen 2004; Schneider 2000).

MIGRATION EXPERIENCES THROUGH THE EARLY TWENTIETH CENTURY

Not all of the groups that entered the U.S. were greeted equally, as clearly noted in the opening quote from Roosevelt. Certainly, not all immigrant groups had the same experiences once settled in the U.S.

Nevertheless, there are some groups that have come to hold an important place in U.S. life and culture, including the Irish, Germans, and Scandinavians who arrived in North American during the nineteenth century.

The Irish established themselves in the Northeast and around Boston, Philadelphia, and other industrial towns where they could find work. The number of Irish entering the U.S. swelled between 1845 and 1849 as the Great Irish Famine destroyed their country and its rural economy (Glazier and Tepper 1983). Many Irish immigrants benefited from understanding English. Yet they were treated as outsiders and endured discrimination that grew from, or was based upon, their religious identities as Catholic in the larger Protestant U.S. Their community was misrepresented as violent, alcoholic, and with little regard for the rule of law. Anbinder captures the difficulties facing the Irish and quotes Oscar Handlin, who describes the Irish immigrant community in his 1959 work *Boston's Immigrants*: "For a long time they were fated to remain a massive lump in the community, undigested, undigestible" (Anbinder 1992).

Germans also settled in large numbers throughout the Midwest of the U.S. in the nineteenth century, although their travels to the U.S. date to the country's early colonial history and the settlements of the Palatines in Pennsylvania (Luebke 1999). The early-arriving Palatines and later more heterogeneous German immigrants were able to establish themselves quickly in urban centers as well as rural farming communities, where they shared a language, religion, and political traditions even as they assimilated to general U.S. cultural patterns and the use of English.[1]

Scandinavians filled farms and small towns from the upper Midwest to the Northwest of the U.S. Janet Rasmussen mentions one Norwegian who came to the U.S. following ethnic networks that originated in his home: "Rather than 'freeze for five dollars a month in Minnesota,' Kofoed [the immigrant reported on here] tried his luck on the west coast and relied upon co-ethnics to access work" (1993:91). And of course everyone crowded into New York City, including Chinese immigrants, who helped to build the modern city and its traditions even as they faced intense pressures from the surrounding community (Lee 2007).

In England, a similar pattern of mobility led to rapid growth in the country's foreign-born population, although some of the foreigners (the Irish and Scotch, for example) did not have to travel far (Wareing 1981). In any event, while the Scotch and Irish flocked to London and the prospects of jobs, indentured servants moved through the city as a first step on the way to the Americas and West Indies between 1683 and 1775. Peasants from the English countryside and immigrants from throughout Europe as well as citizens of regions dominated and controlled by the expansion of the British Empire also arrived in large numbers to work in growing industries and serve London's population growth.[2]

These migrants left hometowns and homelands not to find an adventure or even to explore new opportunities. Rather, they left their hometowns because they were drawn in by business, industries, and commerce that demanded their presence. Yet to assume that labor economics at the point of destination drove the decisions of migrants does not acknowledge the struggles that movers often faced as they traveled and settled. In his work on the history of migration in West Yorkshire, King (1997) notes that the motivations behind migrations were diverse. While the typical pulls of labor, industry (largely cloth mills), and work attracted immigrants, others movers came to Yorkshire only to register the births of their children. These migrants visited Yorkshire and quickly returned to their original communities, hoping that their children might decide to return as citizens and access better positions. A third group also moved to gain advantages for their children and stayed in Yorkshire even though they often found themselves in conflictive situations with few opportunities to join the region's workforce. These situations often translated to only limited success by the migrants, and most non-native immigrants found they could not gain socially in their new homes. King also notes that even as immigrants struggled to find a life and establish their homes in Yorkshire, kin networks linked to sending communities played an important role; these were central to negotiating everyday life, particularly when parish and community resources were closed to most outsiders (1997:294). In other words, as migrants entered and settled in Yorkshire, they depended upon sending families and origin communities to survive and thrive.

Once migrants arrived in their new homes, whether England, the United States, or elsewhere, there was an assumption that the mover would embrace his or her new world and culture and, to paraphrase Theodore Roosevelt, learn the language or leave.[3] There was assumed to be little room for the migrant who would not embrace his or her new home and little patience for the migrant who would not learn a new language. Researchers, as we have noted, assumed that people followed markets[4] and that they were "absorbed" by industries that required their presence (Ravenstein 1889). In this model was an assumption that migration was a natural phenomenon (or another stage in the continued story of the development of our species) occurring where labor shortages caused short-term gaps in national economies. In other words, exogenous forces defined migration outcomes.

Ravenstein's "Laws of Migration," published in 1889, was one of the first attempts to define a coherent framework for the analysis of human mobility. He envisioned migration as a linear process that followed a set of seven basic rules (or laws) and took place within concrete boundaries and between well-defined origins and destinations (for Ravenstein, rural Englishman, Scotsmen, and Irishmen settling around London). First, and most critically, migration followed universal "currents" that were directed by forces of commerce and industry and "absorbed" migrants as workers. In other words, migrants (and in fact even natives) were little more than passive figures directed by forces well beyond their control. They filled jobs that were created by businesses and in return, commerce and industry rewarded them with wages and opportunities that were not available locally.

Ravenstein also assumed that migration was a largely local affair, an easy supposition given the lack of communication technology and the limits on transportation technology in the 1880s. A second rule of migration demanded that its growth would follow a set pattern. Businesses first absorbed those individuals who lived nearby and recruited nonlocals only after exhausting local worker pools. Third, processes of absorption—or the pull, if you will, of business and industry—contrasted in a direct and equal way with the dispersion of individuals from the hinterland.

The fourth, fifth, and sixth rules of migration restate in part the central tenets of Ravenstein's first three rules. Migration produces a direct and equal countercurrent (in other words, a decline in the sending community's or region's population); migrants traveling long distances tend to prefer commercial and industrial centers (or, the pull of labor opportunities drove migrations); and urban dwellers are less involved in migration than are their rural counterparts (assuming urban areas have more and better-paying jobs than do rural locales).

Finally, Ravenstein argued that females were more typically migratory than males (1889:198–199). And while contemporary movement often bears out his belief (women are moving in ever-larger numbers and often outnumber men as migrants), he based this assumption on the demographic structure of English society in the late nineteenth century, a time when Ravenstein found that women outnumbered men. He argued that because there were more women, and because those women could not find husbands, they typically migrated to nearby industrialized towns to find work (1889:196).

The assumption that commerce, business, and industry drove migration—or put another way, that commerce, business, and industry in points of destination absorbed migrants—would seem a clear pathway toward the definition of global migration, its growth through the Industrial Revolution, and the expansion of the United States and markets in Europe through at least the first half of the twentieth century. Yet the reality of migration's growth is much more complex. First, because we are talking about a global phenomenon, we cannot assume that what works in Europe holds true in, for example, Southeast Asia. Second, the demographic structures and cultural practices of various countries and their various populations are not uniform. Third, economic practices vary from place to place and among the differing strata of a country. Bade (2003) points out that European migrants differed in destination, employment, family circumstance, and religious beliefs or ethnic makeup; this is perhaps true for most other countries as well. The economic practices that characterize their home regions as well as the structure and nature of the sending households of which they were members are other distinguishing markers of migrants. Heyman points out that immigrants often suffer economically in new destinations as they accept lower incomes in the hopes of accessing cultural and social opportunities not necessarily available to them in their sending communities (2007). Finally, not all migrants come from free and mobile backgrounds; there are indentured migrants, refugees, and forced migrations that create, a very different set of challenges and outcomes for movers.

When we think about migration in the early decades of the twentieth century we must remember that it was marked not only by economic opportunities and the absorptive powers of newly industrializing states, but also by the particular patterns of each country, their economic structures, and their transnational linkages as well as their political and religious identities (see Gerstle 1999). And while historically movers lacked the technologies that support contemporary migrants and facilitate mobility and communication across borders and between origin and destination communities, migrants past and present have relied upon flows of information, families and friends at points of destination, and shared cultural traditions to ease their integration into their new homes. In other words, just as today we find Mexicans who rely on the information flowing between origin and destination communities to support mobility, in the past migrants followed family and friends to established communities and work; once settled, immigrants often organized themselves around traditional practices that included shared language, specialty foods, and ethnic festivals (Paerregaard 2008).

We have argued that a focus on mobility allows us to move away from the artificial divisions that often separate international migration from internal moves and economic from cultural decision making, and here we return to this concept as a way to explore the relationship or role that internal migration played in the growth of international mobility. Our argument is based on the knowledge that while millions of migrants have moved around the globe, many more have traveled internally, following long-established pathways or perhaps establishing patterns of movement that continued for decades, sometimes into the present day. For many movers, travel to an internal destination was also a first step toward crossing an international border. One can say it is an early stage of the process of developing skills for international migration.

Two forces encouraged mobility (whether internal or international) through the nineteenth and twentieth centuries: the pulls of agriculture, which demanded fresh, strong hands, and industry, which required workers. There were countervailing forces as well; nations sometimes organized to limit migration, as Germany did in the late nineteenth century. Nevertheless, such policies were not easy to set in place, nor did they hold up against the forces of economic change (Wagner 2006). A demand for agricultural laborers drove internal movers in many countries and attracted international sojourners throughout the world to developing destinations.

Europeans, first from the north and later from central and southern regions, left for the fields of England, the U.S., and South America among other places in large numbers. By the start of the twentieth century, the foreign-born comprised about 20 percent of the total population in the U.S.[5] In England, the growth of industry attracted thousands of migrants, and while internal movers were the norm, the demographic map of the country was redrawn. Other migrants headed for South America, specifically to Argentina's agrarian economy as well as the growing cities of Latin America, including Buenos Aires, Sao Paulo, Mexico City, and Santiago, among others places (see Mörner and Sims 1985).

Not all movement driven by agriculture was the same. In the U.S. a demand for farm labor as well as access to farmland encouraged internal patterns of movement as the Midwest and West opened to settlers, many of whom had entered the country as migrants and relocated to new regions (see Kulikoff 1992). Yet, even as the U.S. expanded in part through immigration, enslavement brought millions of Africans to the U.S. against their will and with no opportunity to participate in the social growth of the nation.

Agricultural work attracted many migrants to places where there was demand. European farms had always attracted immigrant agricultural labor in a seasonal fashion. Central and Eastern European migrants arrived in large numbers as seasonal farm workers in Germany and the U.K. Though they were often paid low wages, they were able to earn substantially more than if they had stayed in their origin communities (Hoggart and Mendoza 2000). In larger countries, long distances were covered by some migrants to find work in agriculture. In Turkey, for example, every summer thousands of Kurds from the southeast (near the Iraqi border) traveled about 300 miles to find work harvesting hazelnuts in the coastal towns of the Black Sea in the north (Harm 1985), and many thousands moved to work the cotton fields of Cukurova on the eastern Mediterranean coast (Ozbekmezci and Sahil 2004).

In Latin American, debt peonage systems known as the *Repartimiento* (including *engache* in southern Mexico) moved people throughout the region, including Peru and Bolivia. Coffee *fincas* in Guatemala and plantations in the Caribbean depended upon coerced and forced labor. Locals often joined regional movers and left their home communities (through threat of death or imprisonment) to work fields and to fulfill contracts that typically only further indentured them to landholders (Shlomowitz 1990). Even free movement could change a country, its environment, and its social organization. In Venezuela, a coffee boom in the highlands beginning in the late nineteenth century resulted in a directive by the state to bring in Europeans and develop opportunities in the region.[6] The coffee industry usually attracted internal migrants from impoverished, highland Venezuelan communities. International movers from Colombia found themselves working in difficult situations and for little money while the Europeans who arrived were not particularly interested in farming and instead abandoned coffee and turned to commerce (Price 1994). And while at a macro-level the impacts of the growth of the coffee industry brought a good deal of wealth to Venezuela, it did little to change the structure or makeup of local society. In other words, rural and peasant workers who moved to access jobs in the coffee fields did not see their fortunes rise. Furthermore, the ecology of the coffee plantations promoted diseases that were new to the region, delaying times of marriage as well as the birth of children (Price 1994).

THE GREAT DEPRESSION
AND ITS AFTERMATH

Migration grew throughout the end of the nineteenth and into the early twentieth century. And while such growth was perhaps predicted by Ravenstein and therefore expected, its sometimes unique patterns and structures and the impact of the Great Depression were not.

Mobility did not follow a single recipe. Rather, while it built upon the traditions of internal and international movement, it did so in new ways and with new or at least unfamiliar populations. Working in Botswana, Cockerton (1996) discovered that traditional depictions of women and migration missed the complex and dynamic nature of internal movement. Rural Tswana women were not passive, nor were they following their husbands to South Africa and the jobs they had found. Instead, Tswana women organized strategically to escape the pressures of patriarchy, and to gain access to new economic opportunities in their homeland but also in South African cities. Through these moves they escaped violent and conflictive family life. They also created a new sense of identity and self-worth as they became business women and put aside their traditional roles as victims of domestic violence or a disappearing spouse, or as helpless widows once alone.

The Great Depression brought a good deal of international movement to an abrupt end and led to forced repatriations across the globe. Nearly 300,000 Mexicans were deported from the U.S. to their native homeland and the first Bracero program was abruptly ended (and see Zolberg 1999:75). In Europe, the depression and growing tensions among nations (particularly around Germany) led to state intervention in migration, and the establishment of strong controls over migration outcomes, and in some cases (largely around the building stresses of war and social unrest) forced labor migration (Gibney and Hansen 2005:425).

The growing involvement of the state in migration increased as national economies struggle and nativistic, anti-immigrant sentiments built during economic recession and depression. Yet the Great Depression did not stop migration alone. Mobility declined as nations organized to freeze internal movers, restrict borders, and limit international movement (see Massey 1999). Changes were felt not only in wealthier, Western countries (England, France, Germany, and the U.S.) but also throughout the developing world. The shifts were not necessarily written into policy, but because of de facto policies, inaction, and ineffective programming. In Egypt and Turkey rural-to-urban movement plummeted throughout the years of the Depression as internal mobility declined. It was only from the 1950s onward that rapid urbanization and explosive population growth changed the social geographies of these countries (Gedik 2003). Rural folk remained isolated, while urban dwellers muddled through the effects of the economic collapse (see Rothermund 1996:81).

Internal mobility also shifted from a search for opportunity to an attempt to escape from insecurity, disaster, and danger. Gregory (1989) describes the migration connections that assisted nearly 500,000 "Okies" who left the Dust Bowl of west-south-central Oklahoma for California in the 1930s. These were people not looking for opportunities, but using their ties to family and friends who had already relocated to find work and a better environment. Jesse Carter [pseudonym], who had come to California from Oklahoma in 1936, analyzed the process.

> All "this kinsfolks business," this writing back and forth
> between relatives, he explains, "gits the folks back home to
> talkin' that work is pretty good in California, so they decide
> to pull up stakes and come." Another newcomer confirmed
> the pattern. "We come to Wasco because times were bad in
> Arkansas, and my cousin wrote us that things were pretty
> good out here." (Gregory 1989:27)

MIGRATION IN THE POSTWAR ERA

The coming of the Second World War began a new chapter, one of mobility. What was rooted in human expansion and later in largely agricultural and labor migrations of the nineteenth and early twentieth centuries now was intimately linked with industrialization, national politics, and culture; for the first time, human migration gained a truly global identity. In other words, around the world and in diverse places, people were moving for a variety of reasons and moving in large numbers. Many people moved to access new industrial opportunities within countries and internationally. The numbers of refugees—forced to flee their homes for economic, geographic, and social reasons—grew enormously as the impacts of the war, forced migrations, and intense human rights abuses spread throughout the world (Manning 2005).

Perhaps the most important shift in migration in the years around the Second World War was the rise of forced migration (see, for example, Boshyk, Isajiw, and Senkus 1992; Hirschfeld 1984; Lavenex 2001). While there are many causes that drive forced migration, the outcomes are the same: the goal is to remove one population (often described by local leaders as an undesirable population) and to "cleanse" that region for another population (McAdam 2008). The basis of most forced migration is found in state politics, institutionalized racism, and misguided development, among other things. Around the time of World War II, forced migration was perhaps most obvious as the Soviets moved people deemed undesirable to Gulag camps and the Nazis removed ethnic and religious minorities to labor and concentration camps in an effort to create a sense of national, racial purity. Nevertheless, less intense armed clashes along with wars in many countries such as Turkey, Iraq, and the Sudan in the 1990s and 2000s have forced select groups (e.g., the Kurds) to flee their homes internally and internationally (Demir and Zeydanlioglu 2010; Sirkeci 2005, 2006b).

"Forced migration" describes human mobility in response to a high level of human insecurity, which threatens livelihoods and is accompanied by fear of persecution (Turton 2003). The Web site "Forced Migration Online" describes it as "a general term that refers to the movements of refugees and internally displaced people (those displaced by conflicts) as well as people displaced by natural or environmental disasters, chemical or nuclear disasters, famine, or development projects" (FMO n.d.). However, the term covers a wide variety of human mobility, and thus there are many definitions (e.g., Mooney 2005). These are the movers who are often described as refugees,[7] asylum seekers, and internally displaced people. What refugees, asylum seekers, and internally displaced people share is their history of forced relocation. Most often they are taken from relatively secure homes and lives and forced into situations that leave them with few opportunities to practice their traditions or partake of their culture. As the system that drove refugees out of their homes collapses—as the Nazi regime fails, or the Japanese occupation of China fades—those left behind become refugees. Refugees are mobile, like the migrants we have reviewed. However, where most migrants are making decisions about where and when they go, and while many have ties to family in points of origin and destination, refugees have almost nothing.

Asylum seekers (often unrecognized as refugees) are in a more difficult position as they are often forced to prove that they have been subject to terrible treatment in their countries of origin. "Toughened" immigration and asylum policies in place in most receiving countries contribute to one of the most striking human tragedies of this new century: asylum seekers live in limbo and are often kept at detention centers without access to facilities that are taken for granted by the receiving population (Kalhan 2010). This lack of resources and the sense of loss that often defines displaced people challenge us as researchers but also as humans.

Massey (1999:34) points out that refugee movement, unlike industrial migration, is "not tied strongly to the rhythms of economic growth and development." Nevertheless, refugees are cultural beings and part of the struggle facing the refugee is to rebuild his or her world. This is not easy when homes, lives, and traditions are destroyed, yet refugees struggle to reorganize themselves. Some return to their homes, while others restart their lives anew. A third group relies upon its mobility and seeks security in a new home. These asylum seekers may travel the world looking for the right destination. Some will access Western nations, including progressive countries in Northern Europe (Denmark, Sweden, and Norway) or the United States, where many asylum seekers can find co-ethnics (Crépeau et al. 2006). The challenge for asylum seekers is to find their lives amid the shifts that are happening around them. This was clear in the refugee crisis of 1938, when Germany invaded Austria. In 1938 Jews were expelled from Austria and left at the Hungarian and Czechoslovakian borders. Hungary and Czechoslovakia then forced these refugee movers back to Austria, where they were imprisoned by the Nazis (Safrian 2001).

Today the situation is not the same, but forced migration clearly remains quite brutal (Zetter 2007). On the borderlands of Europe, undocumented migrants, would-be asylum seekers, and refugees are moved, removed, and repatriated by a variety of patrol officers. In recent times Turkish newspapers have been full of such stories of asylum seekers sent back and forth by Turkish and Greek officials because they do not fit the policies of the E.U. or Turkey (see Yaghmaian 2005).[8]

Migration entered a new phase of growth in the 1960s and beyond. Rural-to-urban migration accelerated within countries as cities grew and work became plentiful (Jenny 1984). International migration between countries grew as well, but in ways quite different from the past. While the nineteenth century saw movement from Europe to the U.S. and from European cities to the rural farmlands, now international migration was shifting. Movements were from the Third World to the First, from south to north, or from east to west. Latin Americans began to cross into the U.S.; Southeast Asians traveled to the homeland of the British Empire and set up shop in England, while North Africans found a new home in France—their former colonial ruler.

CONCLUSIONS

In the next two chapters we focus on two dimensions of movement. First we examine patterns of internal migration and ask how it has changed in the last thirty years. Next, we move on to international migration and explore its growth and development. We want to make a few points here before concluding.

Our goal in this chapter has been to capture just a bit of the diversity that is found over time in the development of human mobility and migration. We have purposefully not set out to write a coherent history of migration—we leave that for the historians—but we have tried to emphasize how issues of security and insecurity, belonging, and connections all influence migration outcomes. Movers are not the same: they come from different backgrounds and bring different skills and resources to the challenges of mobility. We must consider the relations of the mover to her or his household, to her or his destination, and to the governments and people of the nations he or she is destined to join, even if for only a moment. What is clear is that the resource-poor migrant, the migrant looking for an opportunity, is in a situation quite a bit different from the mover who has resources, knows where he or she is going, and can get there and succeed.

We began this chapter with a quote from Theodore Roosevelt; even though it has been nearly a century since he made his statement, we still hear the voices of anti-immigrationists around the world demanding that immigrant groups return home or, if they chose to stay, to give up their pasts, languages, and homelands in an effort to become like everyone else. In the United States nowadays, the Minute Men insist that they will secure the U.S. border and defend the country using any means necessary against "unlawful and unauthorized entry of all individuals, contraband, and foreign military."[9] Criticizing the current climate in Britain, Roy Hattersley, an MP in a predominantly Muslim minority neighborhood, said, "Muslims are accepted in Britain—but only if they cease to behave like Muslims." The voices of the anti-immigration movements throughout the world remind us of the challenges that continue to face international movers as they seek new opportunities. Yet there are examples that are not necessarily sad and the stories people tell reference perceptions of human insecurity that may or may not lead to migration as a strategic option.

Three

CONTEMPORARY MIGRATION

Commuters and Internal Movers

Going out to Dagong is not a long-term solution. After several years, I'll return to farm. I would like to find non-farm work in the countryside, but I am not sure what exactly I will do. I have no desire to move the whole family out from the village [to the city]. . . . My wife has to take care of the children at home and cannot join me in migrant work. I cannot take the children with me. School is too expensive in Zhangjiagang [Jiangsu]; the fee is twice what we pay at home.

—A MIGRANT CONSTRUCTION WORKER
FROM RURAL CHINA

Let us take you to several places and briefly introduce the traditional populations you might encounter. Picture a family living in northern China in the Mongol Autonomous Region.[1] Their home is a small hut, and they own very little beyond the few animals they raise, a radio, and some kitchen utensils. Quickly we switch to the highlands of central Guatemala. Chickens scurry around a small hut made of adobe bricks and cane. There is a little field of maize growing and the noise of the community all around. No one has a car, no one has a phone, electrical service is spotty at best, and there is no running water. We jump again, and now we are on the South American Altiplano (the region of high Andean plateaus). Above the tree line the world seems quite desolate and gray. And the people who live here look as poor as their landscape. There are few jobs and few resources to be found. Jump a fourth time, and we are now in Zimbabwe. Families farm small plots of land, scratching a living and hoping for good rains. Finally, flying north, we come to South Asia and the coastal plains of the Indian Ocean. Bangladeshis build their homes on land that is flooded annually. With little to do and few resources to hold, Bangladeshi families farm or work when they can to survive.

Here are five examples of peasants from around the world: northern China, central Guatemala, the Altiplano of South America, Zimbabwe, and the coastal plain of Bangladesh, and five examples of people living in different, but extremely poor locales. These people—some rural poor, some indigenous, and some both poor and indigenous—are the people that we (as Westerners) often think of as conservative, traditional, and followers of practices that are rooted in ancient times. In the present we think of them as representatives of a past we do not know, and as we study these groups in their unique and idealized mythical pasts it becomes ever harder to understand how they live in the present.

When we think about a Mongol living in northern China, our image likely comes from a story we heard in elementary school of the Mongol empire and the world it dominated. At its height the empire controlled much of Asia, yet by the fourteenth century it had begun to collapse, and of course today it lives on only as a legend of a past place. The Maya of highland Guatemala also fill a fictional slot for most of us. They are the descendents of one of Mesoamerica's "high" civilizations. When we think of the Maya of the past, we think of pyramid builders, of temples rising from the jungle (like Tikal and Palenque). This is a world filled with warriors and priests. Today's Maya are poor maize farmers who make their living by working limited fields.

We meet yet another mythical group when we turn to the peasants of the Altiplano. These are the people whose ancestors were part of the Incan empire, a unified political, social, and economic system that dominated the Andes of South America and only faded with the arrival of the Spanish in the sixteenth century. Yet where is the empire that defined the Altiplano? We might think it has gone the way of Great Zimbabwe, a city that dominated southern Africa, controlling trade throughout the Middle Ages and remaining independent until the arrival of European colonialists in the nineteenth century. Today Great Zimbabwe's historical importance and centrality are nothing more than a footnote to a contemporary story of a region whose empire collapsed and whose citizens, now impoverished, have few opportunities and struggle to survive. Finally, we come to Bangladesh, a place that is often described as nothing less than a disaster. As Western outsiders we wonder why anyone would live in such a setting. It is poor, there are no opportunities, and the population must struggle with a difficult environment and seasonal disasters. Yet Bangladeshis know their world is much more. Settled more than four thousand years ago, the region was at the heart of several empires; with the arrival of Sufi leaders in the twelfth century, it was from here that Islam spread throughout Asia.

It is easy to think of northern China, the highlands of Guatemala, the Altiplano, Zimbabwe, and Bangladesh as historical footnotes to the present day and the challenges that human populations now face. This is in part because the mythic qualities of these historical places are powerful. We tend to think of them as part of a larger dialogue on the very development of modern humanity. The Mongols, Classic Maya, Inca, Zimbabweans, and Bangladeshi are all central to the stories about the "rise" of civilization. Their stories frame ideas about how we went from passively living on the landscape to becoming leaders and drivers of world change. The Mongols organized the steppe of Asia and brought new ways of thinking about that world and social life. The Classic Maya brought science, astronomy, and organization. The Inca were able to organize thousands of square miles, encompass ethnic diversity, and harness economic specialization to build a complex state. Great Zimbabwe served a similar purpose in southern Africa, unifying disparate groups into a more complex whole with strong trade and market ties, while the empires of Bangladesh played a central role in the dissemination of knowledge and Islam throughout the region.

But look at the remnants of these empires and civilizations. What we find are people who are marginalized, rural, and poor. To outsiders, the myths of their ancestors permeate the present day and can leave us with the sense that the people we have encountered on our quick, global journey are simply the weak shadows of a glorious past and have little to offer the modern world with which we are concerned. Certainly there is little that these people have to offer us in terms of a study of mobility and migration. While the histories of these groups likely include some mobility (empires, by definition, must conquer others), there is an assumption that at the present we are looking at nothing more or less than nonmovers and isolates, people who live in the past and follow traditions that have little meaning or value for the present.

One of the goals of this chapter, however, is to define the mobility of modern-day populations regardless of their status. Today's mobility is rooted in the past and follows patterns that were established long ago although it might look quite unique and exceptional today. Think of it this way: a Mongol warrior on his pony, riding through a landscape that fears him, is quite removed from a northern Chinese peasant on a train to a large central Chinese city for a factory job that promises to pay more than what can be earned by simply staying home. Yet both are mobile. Consider the Zimbabwean refugee working in the Republic of South Africa. No longer the person at the center of a complex trade and market system, the Zimbabwean is now marginal and often looks to enter South Africa with the constant concern that he might be arrested as an illegal alien in a foreign place. Yet for all of these changes, to understand these populations we must explore the meaning and value of mobility, as it remains central to each population's situation.

We have argued that mobility develops over time and in relation to many factors. Mobility reflects and depends upon the strengths and weaknesses of the individual mover and her or his gender, education, experience, and the like. Mobility also reflects and depends upon the strengths and weaknesses of the household and the resources it holds, the wealth it controls, and the social connections it maintains. In addition mobility depends and reflects upon a community and region and the very migratory history that community and region hold. Finally, we cannot forget the power that national and international law, labor markets, and other such factors have for migration outcomes.

In this chapter we focus on internal mobility and draw a somewhat arbitrary line around the nation, asking what it means to move within the boundaries of the state. Certainly there are many migrants who begin their sojourns within a nation-state, but then move on to cross national borders. These migrants follow a typical step pattern in their movement that is found in many settings (Massey et al. 1998). For our purposes and for this chapter, we cannot forget that the step-migrant often begins his journey within the boundaries of the nation-state but may never venture further.

We organize this chapter around the issues that confront internal movers. We begin by framing internal mobility and the various paths that people take. We also look at the motivations that have led to internal migration since the 1960s and the importance that internal labor markets play. We follow by focusing on the qualities of the mover and the mover's household that encourage internal migration. Next this section explores the contests that drive internal movement, the role played by economic inequality within a nation, and the importance of tradition and sociocultural beliefs in decision making. Finally, we ask about conflicts, which often drive migrants across international borders and can also encourage internal migration; here we focus on those confrontations that encourage internal sojourns.

FRAMING INTERNAL MIGRATION

Internal migration, while not as well defined an area of study as international migration, is the most prevalent kind of move.

Understandably, internal mobility/migration intensity[2] is generally higher than international migration intensity (Bell and Muhidin 2009:18–22). The United Nations estimates that a majority of movers in the developing world follow a path that takes them from a rural origin to an urban destination. They are internal movers (U.N. 2006), and those movers follow fairly set paths from rural communities to cities, urban centers, and the promise of jobs. Internal mobility can comprise actions as simple as commuting or traveling between home and a nearby place of work or as complicated as traveling thousands of miles and over a long period of time (as occurs in China) with the hopes of gaining opportunities that are not present at home. Often internal migration seems more likely to involve people living in smaller and poorer geographical and social units, such as between parishes in Portugal, districts in Panama, or municipalities in Canada (Bell and Muhidin 2009:20).

Commuters are not typically defined as migrants. In fact, sometimes researchers will separate commuters from migrants as a unique and fundamentally different group, arguing that commuting between contiguous locales creates an important alternative to migration (see Muellbauer and Cameron 1998). Put another way, migration emphasizes the mobility of a group over space and time; commuters, on the other hand, are thought of as relatively immobile and tied to a fairly circumspect region. In fact, the relative availability of labor, of opportunities, and of affordable housing encourages commuting locally and should mitigate the need for migration. And local labor and housing markets as well as opportunities can keep movers near their natal home as they avoid long-term sojourns and the costs they may impose. Nevertheless, commuters are moving and their mobility is critical to their well-being.

The commuter does not transcend internal boundaries or international borders and, perhaps most importantly, tends not to challenge traditional models of behaviors. Commuters fill traditionally defined categories rather than opting for new or unplanned kinds of opportunities. Moving locally and within locally defined sociocultural systems, commuters find work that does not challenge what might be expected as normal (and see Renkow and Hoover 2000). Nevertheless, they still demonstrate patterns similar to those of migrants, and their "life-spaces expand with age and repetitive moves from an integral thread that weaves spatial patterns across the life course" (Bell and Muhidin 2009:1).

Like all movers, commuters are involved in making decisions about mobility that have an impact on their futures. Commutes can be a foundation for migrations, or they can stand as an alternative to leaving. They are based on knowledge and on socioeconomic, gender, and political relations within the commuter's community and in the nation as well (see Miera 2008). Commuters balance their decisions against potential migrations and border crossings and against their own abilities and those of their households as well as social and economic forces. Often we find that a household sends some members across boundaries, borders, and frontiers while other members will commute to local, daily destinations. Sometimes, as in the case of Poles who regularly cross into Germany for work (but return home to their natal country daily), commuting is a response to a country's migration policies and programs for integration (Miera 2008). But it is also part of the broader socioeconomic and cultural settings within which individuals, families, and households devise their lives to respond to opportunities and/or to avoid conflict. Commuting has a give-and-take quality as well. Many people in Slovakia travel to work and for entertainment to the capital of neighboring Austria, an hour's trip (see Kraler and Sohler 2007; Williams, Bal, and Koll 2001), while Germans living in Munich travel for recreation to the border city of Salzburg (see Jordan 2006; Schano 2008).[3]

As might be expected, commuters can be found nearly anywhere, throughout history. In the United States, Europe, and Japan commuting includes the large portion of the population that must travel within a region to find work, education, entertainment, and opportunity in response to the spatial distribution of services, shared cultural beliefs, and the like (Renkow and Hoover 2000).[4] Commuting might be thought of as an alternative to migrating, because it does not push an individual to leave her home for an extended period and does not ask him to abandon everyday practices; but it can become quite a burden as it challenges traditions and fosters mobility. In and around London, for example, commuting lengths have grown exponentially as the region has decentralized and the population that works in the city has spread throughout much of the countryside, reflecting a demand for maintaining a rural lifestyle while pursuing an urban model of employment (Nielsen and Hovgesen 2008). A new term, "international commuter assignments," has come into use in human resource management (Scullion, Collings, and Gunnigle 2007:314) to account for the fact that an increasing number of professionals commute to London from as far afield as Edinburgh (about five hundred miles) and Barcelona (a two-hour flight) alongside others commuting from nearby satellite towns and cities thirty to fifty miles away.

This phenomenon is noted for global cities but is also rather common elsewhere. In the central valleys of rural Oaxaca, Mexico, many local commuters travel to the state's capital from surrounding villages. The city is home to a diverse market that is based largely on tourism but also includes the state's government, institutes of higher education, light industry, and an array of commerce that serves the local population. Oaxaca City is surrounded by dozens of rural communities that are linked to the capital via fairly good roads and a complex transportation system. At the same time, local rural communities lack much economic complexity. Many are still organized around subsistence-based agriculture and limited craft production. This situation—a central urban center that serves as an economic focus for an underdeveloped rural hinterland—has also become a magnet for employment, and the city depends on its rural population for about 10 percent of its workforce (INEGI 2008). Daily commuters spend hours moving between rural homes and jobs or schools.

The moves rural Oaxacans make are also defined by their age, experience, and gender, as is the case in most parts of the world. Women are more likely than men to access low-paying service jobs in the city and work as maids in the city's many hotels. Men often find construction jobs that pay better but are only temporary. Teenagers and young adults access university programs and commute to pursue degrees in business, medicine, and other trades. Many of these children will find jobs in the capital city once they have completed their training. Yet Oaxaca City continues to grow (and its population has well surpassed the 200,000 or so individuals that are official residents), and the rural communities surrounding the city have not disappeared. The relatively high cost of housing in the capital, as well as the challenges of urban living (traffic and crime, for instance) and high food costs, has encouraged commuting rather than settling in the city (Smith 2007).

Commuters in urban centers throughout the world follow patterns that parallel those of rural Oaxacans. Some face quite long commutes that can take hours. Lyons and Chatterjee (2008) report that on average Londoners commute over two hours per day, with the average British commuter spending more than 139 hours per year traveling to and from work. Computer technicians in Mumbai may spend hours on the road to reach their jobs. Doctors working in Manhattan may come from as far away as eastern Pennsylvania, commuting once or twice a week and maintaining a second home near their place of business. Commuting experiences of medical doctors in Britain show the difficulty of the commute and its similarities to migration. British doctors living and working in and around London are commuting long distances because of rotation structures, like their counterparts in other countries. Others are making even longer trips:

> Dr. Robinski is said to have woken at 4 a.m. in Poznan
> [Poland] to embark at 5 a.m. on a four-hour drive to Wro-
> claw airport, where he took a two-and-a-half-hour flight to
> Glasgow [UK]. He then drove to Aberdeen, where he arrived
> four hours later, having been awake for nearly twelve hours.
> After a one-hour break, when Dr. Robinski had a shower and
> a hamburger, he was "ready" to see his first patient at 6 a.m.
> (Cappuccio and Lockley 2008:218)

Dr. Piotr Robinski's story is not unique. According to the German Medical
Association, more than 2,600 Germans doctors are flying regularly to the
U.K. for work (Harding et al. 2005), which means a commute of about 500
miles minimum. So the question here is really where commuting ends and
where migration starts.

Commuters are often thought to follow local routes because they lack
the resources that longer moves often entail (Miera 2008). Yet many commuters depend on local, daily, or short-term moves to build wealth (as we
noted in the example above) and to define social identities. Koenig found
just such a pattern among Malians living in Kita, whose social status is defined by their mobility as they invest in different activities throughout the
region (2005). People in the "Kita zone" use strong multilocal networks
that are linked to familial, class, and ethnic resources to create a diversified
foundation upon which to organize their social identity. In other words,
their social identity is defined by their communities, which are defined
by resources available to access labor and capital in a multitude of places
(Koenig 2005:9). In this setting, the commute is not an alternative to migration, rather it is a move that is strategic; when it is successful, it brings
with it wealth and status.

Historically the situation for commuters was not very different, as
movers accessed opportunities and generated identities through their actions. In England and to a lesser degree Scotland the immobility of the
rural folk is a myth that, as Pooley and Whyte argue, cannot be maintained (1991). Not only are the English quite mobile nowadays, but they
were perhaps even more mobile in the past. In the seventeenth century the
rural and poor in England were moving about along fairly short and regular circuits. Pooley and Whyte (1991) note that there was great diversity
among commuters in England. While some remained quite local, moving
between fields as their work was needed, others traveled to access work
as servants to landed gentry. Often these migrants rotated through jobs as

their own personal schedules permitted. Their commutes were facilitated by family, social networks, and friendships that established ties that could be followed and built upon over time. In fact, the connections between workers and employers would often grow quite strong and last beyond the generations that established them.

Commutes cannot satisfy all the needs and wants of individuals and their households, however, and there are not always local opportunities available. This is the case now and was the case centuries ago. Many individuals therefore choose to leave the local confines of household, community, or region and migrate to a more distant, but nevertheless domestic destination. Internal movers follow complicated routes and for a variety of reasons, and find themselves in myriad destinations. Yet the largest segments of these internal movers are following a rural-to-urban path.

Rural-to-urban migration involves the movement of individuals within national borders and from agricultural hinterlands to growing city centers and new kinds of labor, particularly industrial labor. This is not a new path, but one that became perhaps more established with the arrival of the Industrial Revolution and the shift from an agrarian lifestyle to a more urban approach to living (and see Gümüşçü 2004; Postles 2000).[5] In London, for instance, factory jobs pulled individuals to the city and drove the growth of the urban population. A rural-to-urban move was one that opened opportunities for rural folk who had few local alternatives when deciding on their futures. The allure of the urban center came with the promise of opportunity if not always the reality.

The mover finds her- or himself caught in two kinds of uncertainties as she or he considers moving from rural origins to urban destinations (O'Connell 1997). First, there is the lack of knowledge about what awaits the mover who leaves her or his rural home for a job and life that may or may not prove to be a reality, as he pursues an opportunity to get away from a life circumscribed by an agrarian lifestyle that offers few alternatives. Second, there is the future that awaits the mover regardless of destination. In other words, the mover may have little to lose given the situation he or she is already living in, particularly when that situation is balanced against the prospects for the future regardless of the destination. O'Connell (1997) argues that given this uncertainty, migration is an important option as it moves the individual away from the limited opportunities that exist locally (and that a commuter might access) and holds at least the promise of change.

Many times the internal migrant has no choice in the moves that he or she makes. History is full of examples of forced migrations of one kind or another that occur within a country or region as one group (often defined by religious, political, or ethnic terms) displaces a second group (see Christopher, Pybus, and Rediker 2007). The history of Latin America is replete with examples of forced migrations. Similarly, the war zones of Africa have witnessed brutal displacements. Although the episodes are yet to be uncovered fully, the USSR has surely experienced remarkable examples of population engineering. As a result, former Soviet republics have large Russian minority populations and Russia is a major receiving country. One may claim that the times around the dissolution of empires perhaps represent peaks of such forced internal movements. The end of the Ottoman Empire saw millions of Muslims migrating toward the central territories of Turkey, as the Ottoman army was forced out of the Balkans, Arabia, North Africa, the Crimea, and the Caucasus. Those millions of movers built modern Turkey, which became a major sending country from the 1960s onward. We can now link these internal movements following the dissolution of various empires—the Ottomans or the Soviets—to the international movements in the aftermath. Turkey is still a destination for many Muslims from those former Ottoman territories (Sirkeci et al., forthcoming) while the Russian Federation has received millions of immigrants from those former Soviet countries (see Yudina 2005).

The rural-urban disparity is often described as one of the key forces driving internal or domestic migration, and it is easy to assume that this divide is defined largely by economic opportunities. The argument goes something like this: there are few opportunities for work beyond agricultural production in a rural setting, and because development tends to be focused in urban centers, they are the places where growth is found. That growth is dependent on available labor, and the rural population of a country is looking for work. Rural folk are thus absorbed by or drawn to nearby urban centers as a labor resource and to escape the lack of opportunity they face (Lucas 2004). And while economics likely drives a great deal of internal mobility, there are other factors that influence domestic or internal migrations, including the history of movement within a group, the experiences, status, and abilities of the movers, the expectations of the movers and their households, the status of potential sending households, and the expectations that a domestic group holds for its potential movers.

The history of a community is critical to internal mobility. If a region is a center for some investment and development even though it has a rural setting, movers may opt for commutes rather than longer-distance and long-term migrations. Alternatively, rural settings that include very low opportunity costs for movers, at least in relative terms, can attract movers.

This second possibility is evident in countries that have opened rural frontiers to settlers (Carr 2009). This occurred in the 1970s when the highland rainforests of Chiapas, Mexico, were opened to settlers from other parts of the nation. Over a very short period of time, many thousands of "invaders" entered land that was nominally under environmental protection to establish communities (Téllez 2008; Villafuerte Solís and García Aguilar 2008; Viqueira 2008). In Panama, the same thing has happened as rural, agrarian peasants open parklands for settlement; rather than moving to cities, they established gardens on what was (and is still defined as) state land (Kennedy 2002). In Brazil, the push to open rural lands for settlement is particularly strong and has been more-or-less codified into law to support the establishment of new settlements.

As with international migrants, then, internal movers follow one another over time; thus the paths that were established to rural settings are not necessarily abandoned unless there is a shift that increases the marginal costs of movement and forces the migrants to find a new destination (Santos 2007; Skop et al. 2006).

The experiences, status, and abilities of the movers or potential movers also have a role in internal or domestic migration. Poorer households may seek to send members to a domestic destination as a way to reduce the number of individuals in the household who demand resources as well as to bring at least some limited remittances (Cliggett 2005). Movers from low-status and relatively poor households likely do not have the resources to cover the costs of long-distance and cross-border migrations. These individuals may opt to migrate to urban destinations as an alternative. For some migrants, these moves will be a first step in their continued mobility, as their sojourns will take them across national boundaries after they organize the resources necessary to cover their costs. A relatively wealthier household may also participate in internal migration, yet in this case the moves are driven from a position of strength (usually both social and economic). A first advantage is that the migrant is able to use her or his wealth to define a more optimal destination, a determination that can be based upon the strengths of the mover rather than expectations of the destination. This is clearly the case as highly skilled migrants travel to internal as well as international destinations to fill jobs and build upon their cultural capital (Cornelius et al. 2001). Second, the migrant from a relatively well-to-do household typically has more choices in destinations and jobs (Heyman 2007). Third, the relatively wealthier migrant typically has plans for her or his remittances that go beyond the purchase of consumer goods and covering daily expenses (Carling 2008; Cohen 2005; Conway 2007;

de Haas 2006a; Gammage 2006). We often make the assumption that such moves are atypical and that the majority of migrants are poor and moving from a position of weakness, yet evidence from throughout the world, including China, shows that even as the rural-to-urban movement grows, there is often a reciprocal mobility that carries the well-trained and well-to-do away from their rural homes in an effort to build a nation and create a shared identity (Hansen 2005).

Gender also affects outcomes for internal movers. Many groups fear sending their daughters across international borders and will encourage young women to migrate to a national destination as an alternative (Cohen, Rodriguez, and Fox 2008). The leaders of the sending household make the assumption that an internal move does not pose the risks or threats to personal safety that an international move might.

The expectations of the movers and their households are another consideration. Is a household interested in ridding itself of extra bodies to feed? If so, an internal move may be far more efficient or at least a good bit cheaper than sending a child across a border. And while international migrations hold the promise of relatively high remittances, the internal mover also remits. If remittances are not necessarily central to decision making, an internal destination may be as useful as an international one.

Age is another factor. Older migrants tend to move to areas where the climate is more favorable. In the U.S. it is well known that the Sunbelt historically attracted the old from other parts of the country. Older Europeans from the north of the continent move to the Mediterranean shores of Spain, France, Italy, Greece, and Turkey. Relatively cheaper living conditions are another driver for many pensioners, who seek places where their limited incomes go a little further than home.

The status of sending households and the expectations that a domestic group holds for its potential movers also will influence outcomes. Does the sending household have a specific goal in mind for the migration of its members? If so, this may influence the destination. A household may want a child to learn a trade to ensure the long-term economic health of the domestic group. In such a situation, the household likely will send its migrant member to a national school where he or she can learn a trade, expecting her to return to her natal home and begin to earn a living. If a potential mover is hoping to flee his family, an internal move may not be sufficient and he may have to explore international opportunities. Finally, individual migrations are not discrete exercises, as households tend to pool the efforts of their members and the resources those efforts generate. In this respect, we may find that a household will encourage one member to cross international borders while another is asked to remain within national boundaries.

We often assume that internal or domestic moves are easier to make. The challenges of learning a new language or adapting to a new culture are mediated by the shared traditions of a country. Yet the reality is that internal moves can be quite difficult. They may include great distances, as is the case of rural Chinese from the western regions of the country who travel to the eastern urban centers to access jobs. And while the Chinese government does engage in rural development in an effort to keep rural populations at home (Liang, Chen, and Gu 2002), most movers are traveling to urban destinations. As they travel, some minority groups are challenged to learn a new language, experience a new religion, and establish an entirely new way of living. This is perhaps most evident in the experiences of Uighur migrants, who travel from their central Asian homelands, where they follow Islamic traditions, as an internal minority population that faces a great deal of discrimination (Clark and Kamalov 2004). In response, the movers talk of their eventual return:

> I am still a nonmig. My family and my friends feel the same. City people have houses and jobs there. . . . I won't move to the city. Life is much better in the countryside. Rural people are less complicated. Life is easier here. The city is merely a place to make money. . . . I do not want to live there for a long period of time. After I've made some more money I want to return. (Fan and Wenfei 2008: 222)

In some countries there are regulations restricting mobility. In fact in some places internal movers are more difficult than international migration. The Chinese system of *hukou*, similar to that of Soviet *propiska*, maintains a strict registration system within which employment, housing, and even food supply are tied closely to your legal residence (Ha, Yi, and Zhang 2009). Despite all the restrictions, about one in nine Chinese is a migrant and about 25 million of the total are without rights of residence in their destination community (Fan 2008a; Fan 2008b).

Nevertheless, even smaller moves, like those between places that are literally a few hours apart, can challenge the cultural background of a population. Ethnic and religious minority populations often endure bigotry and intolerance from urban dwellers. This is true for ethnic minority populations in Mexico that travel a few hours to migrant neighborhoods in Mexico City and that must manage internal forms of discrimination

(Hirabayashi 1994). Often religious minorities must balance misunderstandings and intolerance as they move from hometowns to new destinations (Dustmann and Preston 2001).

CONFLICT AND INTERNAL MIGRATION

Throughout this book we insist on using a slightly modified terminology. We refer to *movers* and *mobility* to diminish the weight of the widely used dichotomy of "internal" and "international" migration. Mobility is a response, a reaction. Individuals, families, households, and communities throughout history have responded to opportunities and reacted to difficulties and conflicts. Migration appears as one strategic option among others. Internal migration, in this regard, is not different from international migration. What causes movement to be international or internal is largely the mover's ability and resources along with the geographical limits of the state in which he or she resides. In some countries it is possible to avoid conflict and find better opportunities within national borders. The experiences of Kurdish people are a good example of this practice. Iraqi Kurds fled most parts of Iraq to settle in the Kurdish-controlled north during the 1990s and the early years of this century (Fawcett and Tanner 2002; Ladek 2007; Sirkeci 2005). Other Kurds had moved to the industrial cities in the western regions of Turkey over three decades beginning in the 1970s and in response to armed clashes in the southeastern part of the country (Mutlu 1996; Sirkeci 2000).

The scope of "conflict" is rather broad (see chapter 2), and the reader can easily discern that we refer to any tensions, latent or overt, as conflict. The tensions that play a role in migration decisions can become extreme at times. Increased violence often leads to mass displacements, as in the Kurdish and Iraqi cases and in the aftermath of the 2003 invasion of Iraq by the U.S., which displaced 2.4 million citizens (Ladek 2007). One should bear in mind that—when considered from a culture of migration perspective—these moves, forced or discretionary, are likely to increase the overall propensity for international migration as well.

Tensions in the labor markets (e.g., wage differentials, lack of job opportunities, secondary sector, need for cheap labor) are often referred to as key drivers of migration. Rural-to-urban migration is linked to income inequalities and lack of job opportunities between the origin and the destination. Internal migration becomes an option when those who lack adequate social and human capital face unemployment or expect not to be able to find employment to satisfy their needs and wants. In other words, locals who are likely to lose the contest for jobs in their hometowns will opt to move to another place. Struggles in the labor market significantly influence the migration decision. Income inequalities can also be characterized by divisions reflecting class, ethnicity, religion, age, or gender. Low income is also common in a region where steady migration flows are witnessed, as in the case of the Kurdish regions of Turkey. Kurdish-populated eastern provinces have been constantly at the bottom of the Turkish socioeconomic development levels (Dinçer, Özaslan, and Satılmış 1996)—an indication of poor employment opportunities but also of poor infrastructural investment and provision of health services and education. As Mutlu's (1996) projections indicate, the combined effect of ethnic conflict and socioeconomic underdevelopment produced a massive outpouring of Turkish Kurds from the rural east toward the cities in the west. This has created strong Kurdish minorities in major cities.

Conflict is not limited to the labor markets but also occurs within households, where there are strong tensions, for instance, over gender roles and perceptions. There is a wide gap between expectations and realities in rural and urban China. Many Chinese leave their villages to find work in big cities like Shanghai, Beijing, and Jiangsu. Generally it is the men who make the journey, yet it is the women who are more often able to find work and who are sought by factory owners. This leads to household conflicts as Chinese women migrate to cities and return to their rural hometowns say such things as, "I still want to go out . . . but my husband doesn't want me to go . . . he wants me to help him raise some pigs . . . we have been fighting about this matter" (Fan and Wenfei 2008:223). In such cases the husband is left behind to look after children while the wife works and lives in the city. We argue, however, that even in the cases where men migrate gender conflicts are likely to arise, because in the absence of men, women take charge—and this is not an easily reversible process (Donato, Wagner, and Patterson 2008; Gilbertson 1995; Harzig 2006; Livingston 2006). Though they may not like it, many migrant men see their women gaining power, and upon their return to the household they must renegotiate status and relationships, including divisions of labor and child care.

Sometimes hostilities among individuals or families or households may force people to flee internally or internationally. These fights may arise from disputes over marriage (and "honor killings"), land, or even livestock. In a remote Kurdish village in the eastern Turkish province of Mus, two families recently made an oath not to attack each other anymore. Three decades ago a dispute erupted between families over two cows. The following twenty-nine years of fighting resulted in twenty killings. To escape the violence both families migrated to western cities (Yildirim and Tapan 2008).

In a letter to the editor of *The Independent*, a British daily, Mr. Atterbury wrote from Poland to explain why he had emigrated from the U.K.:

> UK nationals move for reasons related to the quality of life: better climate, less aggression and anti-social behaviour. Many of my acquaintances have moved for the latter reasons, and, if not abroad, at least to *quieter locations within the UK*. They are fortunate enough to have the financial resources to be able to do this. I did so to escape the ever-increasing McJob work culture in the UK. I now work as a lecturer at a polytechnic and earn around £125 a week—not much, but I have a secure, responsible, and stimulating job. I sold my bog-standard terraced house in the UK, and now have a pleasant home in the country with more than an acre of land. Most important of all, *I no longer have to endure the aggressive, drunken, yobbish behaviour* that seems to permeate so many towns in the UK. My students are polite, witty, intelligent and motivated. (*The Independent*, 17 Nov. 2007)

This case shows that migration can also be an individual response to broader issues and conflicts that cannot be addressed or resolved alone. It illustrates that there can exist counterflows, from high-wage to low-wage areas and economics, and that quality-of-life issues sometimes feed into migration decisions (and see Heymann et al. 2009).

Conflict dynamically affects the ways in which migration behavior is shaped and changed. The same perception of conflict could cause either internal or international migration. The choice between internal or international migration comes down to the individual's or household's perception of solutions and where to secure these solutions.

MOVERS, THEIR HOUSEHOLDS, AND COMMUNITIES

Our discussion of internal migration would not be complete if we were to ignore the household. We have argued that migrants are not independent actors, but rather are members of households and communities; these households, communities, and even nations have a profound impact on the outcomes of their mobility. Fan and Wang (2008), in their study of Chinese rural-to-urban migration, vividly illustrate the role of families and households, which they describe as a source of security. Whether it is a source of security or is seeking security, the household has a significant influence on migration decisions. While the decision to migrate is often a personal one, a household can have a profound effect on the reasons for moving, destinations, expectations, and uses of remittances. An individual may want to leave her natal or conjugal home for personal reasons, yet where a household is concerned the personal often comes into conflict with the expectations of others; and while the individual mover and his household may agree over the destination of a move, harmony is not always assured. For example, and as we have argued, a household's leaders may limit the opportunities of young women who are interested in migration, while they may encourage young man to take more risks. As we noted earlier, the case of the Chinese wife whose migration was vetoed by her husband shows how decisions are made and contested within the household. Age, experience, and expectation are critical to outcomes and the experiences and needs of older parents often frame the decisions of their children.

Communities and their histories also have a profound impact on migration outcomes. There are communities, regions, and ethnic minorities that are practiced in domestic migration. In fact, there are often expectations that certain groups will be found at particular internal destinations. For example, in the U.S., African Americans migrated internally from their rural homes in the south of the country to northern cities as the labor market expanded but opportunities in the south did not materialize (Adelman and Tolnay 2003; Hahn 2003).

CONCLUSIONS

For many movers mobility is a local, internal affair. They will cross no international borders, at least not at first. Their initial ventures away from their natal homes will take them to nearby destinations and others within their countries of origin. To assume that these people are immobile is to limit them to a life that is more a part of our fantasy of what the traditional world is like than to acknowledge the realities that characterize the worlds these people know. Humans are movers, as we have seen; it is part of what makes us who we are. For many local, poor, rural, and indigenous people, mobility is critical to survival. If we return to our opening vignettes, we realize that culture groups, even traditional culture groups, are far more mobile and complex than perhaps we had thought. We are cursed by a need to classify people in order to make sense of the world around us. When we classify people as rural, traditional, and indigenous, we often assume they are also immobile. Yet, as we have shown, mobility (and in this case internal mobility) is part of what makes each of these groups modern.

Nevertheless, it is also obvious that there is no clear separation between internal and international mobility in terms of what drives people to move and how they make those decisions. We are security-seeking creatures, perhaps like any other. So we do move around to establish ourselves in places where we perceive security. It could be somewhere, anywhere, where we can earn a little more, or feel more comfortable away from "yob culture and drunkenness."[6] This place may appear within the national borders where we are supposed to belong or just beyond them or even far away. Also it is essential to recognize this is not a one-way process, or a one-off adventure. People move around through their life courses, perhaps for different reasons, and in different ways in different ages.

Four

CONTEMPORARY MOVERS

International Migration

When I got here I was glad to see all the people that came from my place, and they started to make a good time for me. They made a party, and they had wine and biscotti, and lots of meats and macaroni. I was surprised that we had macaroni because I thought that they only had this in the old country.
—LIBERATO DATTOLO, ITALIAN IMMIGRANT WHO ARRIVED IN BRIDGEPORT, CONNECTICUT, IN 1914

My father came to America when I was very young, so I don't really know what he did. In America he worked in what they call a "lardy," a factory, in New Jersey. He lived in a boardinghouse. The landlords were a husband and wife and they were of the same nationality. And one day they said to him, "Martin, you need to get your wife and children over here. We'll lend you the money. And when your wife comes, she can work to help us get boarders in, and you can pay us back." So that's what he did.
—CARA WEICH, IRISH IMMIGRANT WHO ARRIVED IN THE U.S. IN 1905

A few popular assumptions apply to international migration and make understanding the outcomes of international mobility difficult. First, there is the perception that international movement is something new. Second is the assumption that most international movers are poor and fleeing poverty by exercising mobility. Third is the belief that international migrants take jobs and opportunities away from the citizens of receiving nations and in the process drive down wages. Fourth, there is a perception that once migrants arrive in their destination, they will never leave; and fifth, there is the assumption that international migration is best countered by supporting development in the home communities of the very migrants who are driven to cross the border because they are poor and cannot find jobs.

While these assumptions are powerful and show up again and again in the literature and debates and in the popular media, the realities of international migration are really quite a bit more complicated; while we could probably find an example that proves each one of the above assumptions, in reality there is much more support for the following statements. First, international migration is not something new.[1] In fact, the early decades of the twentieth century saw more international movement, at least in terms of the percentages of migrants moving to new destinations. Second, international migrants are not poor, except in relationship to those of us in the West with resources. Migration is a costly endeavor, and the poor in most countries cannot afford to cross international borders. Not only do they lack the money to cover the expense of border crossings, they also lack the social capital (or social ties) that typically support cross-border movement. They may also lack human capital and the experiences necessary to plan for, cope with, and succeed at migrating.

Third, migrants generally take jobs that no one in the receiving area wants to fill; further, as they participate in a destination country's economy, they create additional demands for goods and services that must be met. Migrants can thus have a positive effect as they encourage economic expansion to meet their needs, and, of course, their tax payments (whether through sales taxes, retirement programs, or federal taxes) fill a receiving nation's accounts. Immigrants are almost always a low-cost addition to the qualified workforce in their destination, and employers are usually very happy to exploit them. Fourth, migrants typically do not want to stay in destination countries, but the rules and regulations that define borders and the increasing costs of crossing those borders make it more and more difficult for international movers to return home. The same rules that restrict access often force migrants to settle. The costs of border crossing and fears of arrest make circular or short-term migration almost impossible and so people settle. Finally, while local economic development is a tool we hope will keep people at home, until nations invest in real growth and the integration of migrant-sending regions into national economies, there is little potential for change or development.

Our goal in this chapter is to define international migration, its motivations, and its patterns, and to explain why it is so important not just to movers, but to nonmovers and to the countries they are leaving as well as the countries they are destined for. Finally, we examine the impacts and outcomes of international migration and its economic as well as social and cultural effects.

THE GROWTH OF
INTERNATIONAL MIGRATION

International migration, or migration across national borders, has grown rapidly in the last decades, but it is not a new phenomenon. Moving across national borders freely or by force is a process that dates back generations. Colonial powers forcefully moved populations from one region to another, often enslaving ethnic groups in the process. At the same time, other migrants moved freely, in search of new opportunities. Still other groups fled the economic, social, religious, or political insecurity of one region for another.

We follow Massey et al. (1998) in dividing the history of modern international migration into four distinctive periods: the mercantile period of the sixteenth to the nineteenth centuries; the industrial expansion that followed, from the start of the 19th century to the 1920s; the decline in international migration that followed upon the heels of the First World War and the Great Depression; and post-industrial migration that took off in the 1960s and continues to the present. Each phase brought with it specific qualities and was also defined by winners and losers.

Mercantilism (spanning the mid-sixteenth through late eighteenth centuries) was organized around the control of commodities and the wealth those commodities represented. Sovereign states, particularly in Europe, sought to expand their power and increase wealth through the control of new commodities but also through the control of labor. Mercantile regimes encouraged immigration rather than emigration as a way to attract skilled labor; once these workers were settled, their further movement was discouraged. When religious intolerance led to the persecution of skilled, but non-Catholic labor, England, Holland, and the German states competed for these workers, and went so far as to support the organization of craft guilds to encourage business and control (Isaac 1947:17). While mercantile states discouraged emigration, international movement did occur for three groups of immigrants associated with colonial expansion: colonialists, who traveled with government support to open new regions, find new raw materials and resources, and organize new industries; free movers, who settled in new regions in an effort to expand production or establish local farm economies; and forced migrants, moved against their will to serve colonial and business interests. Isaac points out (1947:17) that early movers comprised a diverse group, including prisoners of war, criminals, and indentured laborers as well as hundreds of thousands of slaves.

While there is an assumption that it was colonialism that drove mercantilism through the seventeenth and eighteenth centuries, anthropologists often argue that it was mercantilism—and its relatively cheap and large migrant pool—itself that drove imperialism and colonial expansion. Sidney Mintz (1985) describes this pattern in his analysis of the growth of sugar production in the Caribbean and its move from a "monopoly of a privileged minority" (1985:45) to a food for the masses. In its expansion, sugar production engaged slave labor, promoted industrialization, and manipulated well-organized supply-and-demand chains to create an integrated commodity that supported the English Crown.[2]

The second group consisted of those "free" individuals who moved in search of new opportunities. This category was divided between those who left with little in their pockets and bargained that opportunities were better in the colonies, and wealthy entrepreneurs who established plantation systems in the Caribbean or, somewhat later, the southeastern seaboard of North America (King and Connell 1999). The third group included slaves—in particular the nearly 10 million Africans who were forcibly taken from their homelands and resettled to work the plantations established by entrepreneurs in the Caribbean, among other places.

Industrialism and the growth and expansion of capital-intensive production models ushered in the second wave of modern migration. This phase was rooted in the shifts in labor and work requirements that came with the arrival of new technologies and the rise of capitalist modes of production. International moves competed with rural–urban migrations (described in the previous chapter) and found populations crossing borders, more-or-less freely following paths to available jobs and opportunities. In Europe and throughout the nineteenth century, migration moved populations from rural settings to cities and to centers of production throughout the region, to the U.S., and to countries throughout Latin America. While the pull of potential work was critical to attracting immigrants to new destinations, just as important were co-ethnic pioneers who had established themselves in new destination communities and countries. These pioneers gave critical support to new immigrants who might not share language or religion with their destination countries. These pioneers often acted as intermediaries for new immigrants, aiding in the negotiation of work, residency, and so forth.

Depression, war, and economic crises throughout the first decades of the twentieth century put a halt to much cross-border movement. In fact, in many places immigrants were forcibly repatriated. For example, laws were shifted in the U.S. and nearly 300,000 individuals were returned to Mexico. Migration rates remained low throughout the Second World War, because the war limited a great deal of free movement. Yet there were programs to cover worker shortages as industries sought labor; for example, the Bracero program brought foreign workers to the U.S. on short-term contracts to fill in for men who had been drafted to serve in the war effort. Nevertheless, in most countries internal production focused on simply putting people to work, and foreigners were often seen as a challenge to internal employees (Cohen 2006; Durand 2007; Massey et al. 1998).

With the end of the war and rapid changes in global economics and politics, migration rates increased once again, primarily for two reasons. First, there was an increase in domestic movement as countries recovered and internal economic growth drove the rural-to-urban flows that we focused on in the last chapter. Growth also drove international movement, as workers began to travel to destinations where they could find jobs and opportunities; unlike the past, however—when skilled laborers were sought and their abilities earned a premium—now migrants were largely unskilled and finding work in the growing service sector (Stark and Wang 2002; Taylor, Rozelle, and de Brauw 2003). Flows tended to track from south to north, as represented most clearly by Latin Americans and Caribbeans traveling to the U.S., and east to west, including movers from Southeast Asia to the Middle East and Europe (Massey et al. 1998).

We may well be in a new phase of migration; the current global economic crises are changing the way capital and labor are organized. The topography of migration and its regulation have significantly changed since the events of 9/11 and the economic recession of 2008 (Fix et al. 2009; Jha, Sugiyarto, and Vargas-Silva 2010; Ratha and Mohapatra 2009). International migration and immigrants are subjects of a complex security debate and increased xenophobia. Tightened security at ports of entry encourages illegal crossing and strains national resources, creating new restrictions and hassles while resolving very little. Perhaps our governments are convinced that there are hidden terrorists among immigrants and travelers. This visceral mistrust of the foreign has increased xenophobia across the board.

While xenophobia rises and borders become more difficult to cross, internal/international disputes create insecurity at home (in Iraq, for example) and lead to new pressures on insecure populations to potentially migrate. In this new period of global crisis the questions surrounding migration become questions about movers themselves and not about states and policies. Put another way, in this period of economic crisis the focus is not on movement (in other words, migration) and what drives that movement but on the mover (or migrant). Popular perceptions blame the migrant for nearly every ill that faces the state. Rising crime rates? Rather than undertaking a reconsideration of legal codes and anti-crime initiatives, blame the migrant, who carries the taint of criminality across borders. Healthcare costs are rising too fast? Rather than an making an honest analysis of the costs and benefits of the current healthcare situation, blame the migrant, who crosses the border to access our dearly won medical system, at no cost to him- or herself. And what do we do about education? Reform is too difficult: it is much easier to suggest that educational resources are being drained away and cannot support the citizens who pay for schools; it is much easier to blame the migrant, whose children clog our schools and either cannot read or speak native languages, adding strains to already overworked staff.

Of course, the reality of migration is far from this caricature. These stereotypes are often based on fabricated data or twisted views promoted by right-wing media after little debate based on reliable research. The overwhelming majority of migrants entering countries like the U.S., England, Germany, and the like are hard-working, law-abiding individuals who seek opportunities that they cannot find at home. They are migrating to support families, earn a living, and continue a life as productive citizens, not as criminals. In fact, there is no correlation between crime rates and migration, and several studies show that the overall decline in crime in the U.S. has occurred even as migration rates to urban centers increase (Chomsky 2007; Terrazas and Batalova 2009). Most migrants are healthy and have little interest in accessing healthcare. In fact, many migrants go without healthcare as it is expensive. Insurance is nonexistent for most movers and many migrants fear that attempting to access healthcare may put them at risk of being caught if they are in a destination country illegally. Often, migrants are physically healthy and of working age. They don't include children or the elderly in their moves. Rather, they prefer to support the elderly in their countries of origin and sending communities. And while they might enter a country with the hopes of funding their children's education, they typically plan to pay for schooling in their sending communities. In other words, one of the goals that brought them across a border is to cover the fees for schools at home (Abu-Ei-Haj 2007; Gamburd 2008; Kandel and Kao 2000).

Not surprisingly, the militarization of borders between countries to combat rising migration rates has not had the outcome supporters of such moves might have expected. Militarized borders and restrictive migration policies were, in their organization, assumed to be effective tools in the reduction of the flow of individuals from sending to destination countries — from Mexico to the U.S., from Northern Africa to Spain and Italy, and from Asia and the Middle East to Europe. In many ways these programs have only made migration a more costly and dangerous move. Criminal syndicates are nowadays far more involved in smuggling individuals across borders for profit (Cornelius, et al. 2008). For example, Mexicans who are interested only in accessing opportunities in the U.S. and North Africans looking only to travel to Europe find themselves involved in the movement of drugs across borders by smugglers and criminal syndicates, which demand their participation as part of arranging their transport across borders.

The rising costs of crossing borders and restrictive employment standards also mean, first, that migrants must stay in destination countries for far longer than they had originally anticipated as they struggle to cover the fees involved in their crossing. Second, migrants remain in destination countries far longer than originally planned for fear of being caught as they try to return to a sending community and country; and third, they sometimes forsake a sending community and bring their families across the border as one way to avoid making these lengthy sojourns without family. Finally, these policies and practices have made destination countries, as well as many sending countries (some of which are weak states), into breeding grounds for illegal gangs involved in lucrative trafficking and smuggling businesses (Garland 2009).

PATTERNS AND PURPOSE

Many people assume that migration is a means by which the poor are able to flee poverty at home. And while our brief history of the growth of international migration suggests that most moves are driven by economic demand and need, a person cannot migrate if he or she lacks resources (Stark 1986, 1991; Stark and Taylor 1989). A response to the assumption that migrants are poor must insist on an understanding of "poverty" as a relative state. To us in the West, living in the U.S., England, or Germany, for example, the people who cross the border—whether from Mexico, Pakistan, or Turkey—might appear poor, but in fact they have more resources than many of their fellows and they are using those resources to reach new opportunities. The very poor cannot afford to migrate, or else can only afford to move to an internal destination rather than crossing an international border.

Contemporary migration then partly involves an economic decision, but it concerns much more. It comprises a cultural decision, a social decision, and even a religious and ethnic decision. Migration must be driven by more than the demand for labor and new forms of production. Nevertheless, economics and labor are assumed to be the keys to understanding migration outcomes, whether the focus is plantation owners in the past, industrialists during the rise of capitalism in the nineteenth and early twentieth centuries, or the service sector of recent history.

Of course the pull of jobs, better living standards, security, and future economic success and the push of a lack of opportunity, economic inequalities, and environmental disasters—among other differences that exist between sending and receiving countries—are critical to migration decisions. The economic motivations that drive migration at a macro-level (in other words, at the national/global level) and also play into decisions at a personal level (or micro-level) are only part of the migration story. Let us be clear: we do not want to ignore markets and economics in our discussion. In fact, understanding the economics of migration is critical to defining mobility. However, a discussion that only notes the economic realities of migration misses the other important factors that drive migration and the ways in which ecology, society, and cultural choices play into the choices of mobility and immobility. The notion of a culture of migration recognizes that mobility is rooted in cultural and social acts. Migration is an economic decision, but not simply that. It is a political decision, but politics is not enough to drive it. Of course, we cannot reduce migration to a cultural explanation alone. We must consider many different forces and factors that motivate movement. We must realize that these factors will work together. And we have to understand that there will be times when they are at cross-purposes. For example, we are in a moment when migration is changing. The relative ease that characterized international moves in the 1980s and 1990s gave way after 9/11 to much more difficulty.

Two questions we must ask are: Why move? Who moves? Migration, particularly international migration, is not a simple undertaking. It begins with crossing national borders and can include moving thousands of miles. International migrants typically do not share a great deal in common with the dominant community in the countries they enter and in which they hope to settle and find opportunity. Migrants may speak a different language, follow a different religion, and participate in a very different social world with its own unique cultural codes. All of the differences that come with crossing borders—from the personal to the cultural, the religious to the economic—make migration hard. Think of a Mexican coming to the United States, who speaks a different language (Spanish in Mexico, English in the U.S.), practices a different religion (Catholicism in Mexico, oftentimes Protestantism in the U.S.), follows a different social code and practices, and is part of an economy that is organized around low-wage work, a weak national currency, and a high rate of graft. Kurdish Turks are in a similar situation in Germany (as are Pakistanis in England), where as non-German speakers they face linguistic hurdles. The Protestantism that is central to German thought and culture characterizes Islam as a religion of terrorists and a social code that is constructed around traditions that are truly foreign to the native-born (see Cohen and Sirkeci 2005 on Mexican and Kurdish parallels). A more extreme example comes from Japan, where migrants, despite having to forgo citizenship, accept second-class status and see little hope for integration, yet continue to enter the country (Douglass and Roberts 2000; Kashiwazaki 2005). Migrants continue to cross borders and seek new opportunities.

International movers are typically wealthier individuals with resources to help them cover the costs of movement. They are not moving to find a handout (and we'd ask just what handouts might a person hope to find in the U.S., for example)—they are moving to find opportunities. While some move to flee insecurity at home, often these movers also have resources to help them manage the costs of border crossing.

One of the best ways to think about international migration is to focus on the movers and to understand the strengths they bring to their migrations. Typically migrants make decisions as members of households.[3] Migrants bring personal strengths and weaknesses to their moves, such as health, education, training, age, and gender, but the households also have an influence on outcomes. Household strengths and weaknesses range from internal and external resources, intra-household labor, time and income, and nonmonetary as well as economic contributors to welfare (Conway and Cohen 1998:30).

Internal and external resources include the labor power, health, ability, and status of the migrant and other members of his or her household. These strengths are defined in relation to both other households and overall national economic patterns. A household with strong resources, as defined by a community, may be of a high-ranking local status, but that status may not translate to economic power. On the other hand, the household with workers employed in and out of the household may hold economic power, but lack local status. In any case, the status of a household economically and its relative rank vis-à-vis other households in a community are a resource that the successful international migrant will likely access to cross a border. Internal resources, including labor, income, ability, background, age, and training, also influence migration outcomes and can frame the decisions a migrant will make. Is a move considered to cover the economic shortfalls of a household, or is a move to support the education of its members? These are very different decisions and are defined not only by the wants and needs of a household's members, but by the very strengths of the household in relation to other households and national economic patterns (Adams 2006).

Finally, both noneconomic and economic contributors to the household can influence migration outcomes. Noneconomic contributors to a household are those individuals who work without pay, or who are involved in nonwage work such as agricultural labor, housework (often described as homemaking), education, child care, and the like. While economic contributors are working for the household and earning wages or salaries outright for their efforts, it is important to remember that sometimes people think of themselves as noneconomic contributors when in fact they are earning wages. These people are generally involved in informal work and their earnings vary from day to day. Women who prepare and sell foods from their homes, for instance, often describe themselves as noneconomic actors and often do not think of themselves as contributors to a household's economic well-being. However, Cohen was able to work with some women participating in the informal economy in Mexico and found that they often earned substantial amounts of money; when their husbands were away and working as migrants, the money these women earned was often the only available cash in the household.

It isn't surprising that a household that lacks economic contributors usually needs to uncover other resources it can access to support the migration of individual members, while households with economic contributors (whether they are employed in the formal sector or are working informally) have opportunities to support migrants in more complete and complex ways. In other words, migrants from households that lack economic contributors and are economically marginal often face a set of decisions that do not challenge movers who are economically better off. For example, the peasant who farms for his household but does not earn money to cover other expenses likely will send a child away to find work as a way to earn the money that is lacking. The household with the most limited economic options has the most numerous choices to make in response to migration outcomes. For example, will remittances be spent on daily expenses or be invested? Typically, the rural and impoverished household cannot invest and must use remittances to cover daily costs of living. To return to our earlier point, the household, not only the individual, frames outcomes for the migrant and influences the decision he or she will make.

To return to the question of what motivates international migration: Despite the discussion above, we would likely argue that the clearest motivations for international migration are economic. But if economics alone rule mobility and motivate migration, we might rightly ask why we don't find more people crossing the border. There is a joke among anti-immigrant groups (among others) that the U.S. must fear the movement of Mexicans across the border because the crossings won't stop until Mexico is empty (or perhaps filled with Central Americans) and every Mexican national is living in the U.S. The reality of migration is that while there are many Mexicans in the U.S., the overwhelming majority remain in their home country. The economic reasons for migration must not be a singly sufficient impetus, as sometimes people don't choose to migrate. We need also to understand the motivations and decisions of nonmovers, or stay-at-homes (this is an issue we cover in the next chapter).

But when we say that economics do matter, what do we mean? It isn't simply that a migrant will earn more money if he or she crosses the border; considerations regarding the decision to migrate are not just economic—they are cultural, social, and political and they are related to and influenced by a mover's status, gender, ability, household, and community—not just economic desires.[4]

LABOR AND INTERNATIONAL MIGRATION

Another concern voiced by critics of migration is that international movers take jobs and opportunities away from a nation's legal residents and in the process drive down wages. The short response comes in two parts, telling us first that migrants do not take jobs away from citizens. Migrants generally fill and work the jobs native citizens will not take. This is particularly true of low-wage, unskilled labor; as we've argued, and as most evidence suggests, in contemporary times it is unskilled labor that attracts most international movers.

While it may be true that wages for unskilled work are marginally impacted by migration, we argue that migrants are not to blame. It is really employers who are suppressing wages. Migrants are filling the jobs that are available; they are not creating jobs or setting wages. Friedberg and Hunt (1995:42) note: "Most empirical analysis of the United States and other countries finds that a 10 percent increase in the fraction of immigrations in the population reduces native wages by at most 1 percent." And of course, everyone believes they are working for less than they are worth (from the richest industrialists to the poorest street sweeper); migrants, like any other group, search for the best wages they can find.[5] Immigrants are not really concerned with suppressing wages, and the jobs they take are the jobs that are offered, not necessarily the jobs they might have at home (Heyman 2007). If this point seems disingenuous, just think about the skilled, trained, and educated immigrant who finds work as a low-wage, unskilled worker. One of the most important differences between internal and international migration is the fact that workers often find the jobs they are trained for if they stay within their country of origin and do not risk crossing an international border. They may not be paid well by our standards, but relative to what others make in their country of origin, a trained worker will typically command a high wage there (Heyman 2007).

A second important point to remember is that immigrants bring money into their destination country. Immigrants have to pay rent and utilities, cover transportation, and put food on their tables just like everyone else. Each of these activities takes resources, and on average an immigrant typically spends 60–80 percent of his income on costs associated with living in the new country. Immigrants also pay taxes, including Social Security taxes in the U.S. (Cohen, Jones, and Conway 2005; Koc and Onan 2004). These are costs that often will not benefit the immigrant, and the Social Security Administration has received millions of dollars from the work of immigrants to the United States.

If migrants do not take jobs from us, why are they in places like the U.S., England, and Germany? Answers include the pull of the market system and the promise of cheap goods, work opportunities, and freedom of expression, among other things. Pull factors combine with push factors within a sending country to motivate cross-border movement. In countries like Turkey, Pakistan, Mexico, El Salvador, Honduras, and the Philippines opportunities are lacking, particularly for rural folks.

Working with the push that comes from a native country is often a very specific pull. Many migrants are recruited to fill specific jobs, and oftentimes national laws are authored to support recruitment and success for certain industries. This is most clear where skilled and highly skilled migrants are recruited to fill specific jobs.[6] Recruiting can be extremely specific and tied to a country or sometimes even a group or gender within a country. A good example of this process is the recruitment of Filipino nurses to fill the increasing shortage that faces healthcare providers in the U.S.[7] Filipino nurses are attracted to the U.S. because of job opportunities and relatively high wages. They also find a large Filipino community in the U.S., one that includes nearly 2 million Filipinos, with more than 1.2 million living in the western states (Semyonov and Gorodzeisky 2008).

While skilled migrants often have opportunities that their unskilled co-nationals lack both at home and abroad, there are several forces that drive the unskilled across national borders. Key are neoliberal reforms that have generally increased the cost of living in sending countries, particularly for the rural poor, who were marginal even before reforms occurred (Gledhill 1995).[8] A lack of internal opportunities does motivate migration. Finally, there are the social and cultural forces that "push" migrants away. Migrating is a rite of passage, something that all young men and a growing number of young women can do. It is also a means to an end: a migrant's sending community and nation cannot always support families, and as landholdings dwindle and agricultural production is challenged by the demand for store-bought goods, localized production declines. Local production can collapse entirely, and in such a situation migration is a way to access the money necessary to live life in our ever more monetized world. Finally, migration becomes a cultural artifact. Co-ethnic communities in points of destination serve as attractors for migrants who are looking for new opportunities and places to settle. Friends and family serve as important social networks as migrants negotiate the border and settle. Without family, friends, and co-ethnics, migration is an extremely difficult process and the decision to attempt it is not an easy one.

MIGRATION, RESIDENCY, AND TRANSNATIONALISM

Opponents of migration reform often argue that opening or easing border-crossing restrictions will allow immigrants to settle in destination countries. They point to the many thousands of Kurds and Turks settled in Germany, Pakistanis settled in England, and Mexicans, Dominicans, and others settled in the U.S. as evidence supporting their point. We do not deny the growth of these minority immigrant populations, yet we would also caution against being too critical. First, global migrations are not new—they were central to the peopling of the Americas and included the movement of ethnic minority groups from European homelands throughout much of the historical development of the U.S. and Latin America. At one level, contemporary movements parallel those of the late nineteenth and early twentieth centuries when millions of individuals traveled from Ireland, Italy, and Germany to the U.S. to seek their fortune. The major difference is that contemporary movers are not joining the ranks of industrial workers as they did in the past. Yet if we look beyond the U.S. and Europe to Latin America, we find that immigrant groups fill important niches as entrepreneurial movers who not only find work in the service sector but engage themselves in nation building.

Japanese migration to Bolivia (among other destinations in Latin America) is a good example of what we mean. Japanese traveled from their homes in Okinawa to southeastern Bolivia under the sponsorship of the U.S. and as part of a broadly constructed resettlement program (Masterson and Funada-Classen 2004). The Okinawan community remained quite small, although over 300,000 Japanese immigrated to Latin America through the twentieth century. Nevertheless, this small group has been economically successful. Although Okinawans manage farms and businesses and are integrated into the national economy, at the same time— and unlike Japanese immigrants to Brazil and Peru—Okinawans are extremely segregated from Bolivian society and continue to maintain strong ties to their hometowns. Perhaps more intriguing, Okinawans' strong relationships with Japan and Japanese cultural traditions exist in spite of the strong discrimination Okinawans have faced in their sending homes and island (Suzuki 2006). For Okinawans in Bolivia, distance works to bridge the gulf that separates them from Japan, but also creates opportunities for economic success that were not available in the past.

As our examples suggest, many of the migrant groups that are settling in new countries maintain strong ties with their families, sending households, and communities, yet they are also often committed to the countries they have joined as new citizens in ways not linked to their legal status. The concept of transnationalism explains how these new immigrants bridge the gaps between their sending and destination communities. "Transnationalism" is used in many different and sometimes conflictive ways, yet at its core it refers to the ways in which migrant groups are able to bridge the gaps between sending and destination areas and remain strongly rooted in both (see Basch, Glick Schiller, and Blanc 1994; Hannerz 1996; Vertovec 2009). Transnational linkages form around cultural, economic, political, and social institutions. They can be popular and constructed around broadly shared beliefs, or they can be limited and organized around an event or practices that are common to only a minority. Transnational ties can be real or they can be imagined. In other words, they exist in the construction of strong social ties between individuals, assisting those individuals in their moves; but they also exist in the shared beliefs and practices that are assumed to define a group. Finally, transnationalism does not apply to all immigrant groups. It is not a force that drives migration, nor is it a factor in all decision making; however, where it does exist, it often aids migrants as they cross borders (Conway 2000).

Migrants express transnationalism in many ways throughout the world. The practiced use of a native language by a migrant in a new destination community is a simultaneously simple and complex transnational expression. The act is simple in that it develops from the innate qualities of the migrant; he or she knows the language he or she was brought up speaking and will continue speaking. Yet it becomes a complex marker of identity, of groupness, and it creates a community for migrants where one might not otherwise exist. Mixtecos, for example, come to Los Angeles, California, from their homes in the highlands of Oaxaca, Mexico, where their native language exists alongside Spanish. Mixtecos invest in the language they know and use it to define themselves as a unique group in the U.S.— a group that may be marginal, but one that is present and can be found through programming on Radio Bilingüe.[9]

More complicated, but no less important, are the cultural linkages that sometimes aid immigrants as they travel from hometowns to destinations in the U.S. and Europe (Paerregaard 2008; Santiago-Irizarry 2008; Scott and Cartledge 2009; Triandafyllidou 2009). Transnational cultural markers may be carried by migrants as they travel to new destinations. They can also be created anew once migrants reach their destinations. Regardless of the process through which a cultural marker is created, its transnational quality is not something planned. Rather, the transnational quality of a cultural marker develops through time as artifacts are transformed to fit the needs of the migrant community.

Paerregaard (2008) uses the example of religious traditions that Peruvian migrants have carried to new destinations throughout the world. Sometimes the traditions are founded upon practices that come with the migrant from her home community. Co-migrants from a specific Peruvian community, for instance, continue to celebrate the patron saint of that community as they establish themselves in their new destination. Sometimes they also adopt and adapt new religious traditions to meet the needs of the moment. In the case of Peruvians, as with other groups, native symbols become tools that "sacralize public space" in the destination community and perhaps even the country and help the migrants make a moral claim as members of a new society (Paerregaard 2008:150). The symbols are not only religious. Food, for example, adds another dimension, one that nearly everyone has experienced. Traditional foods are carried by migrants to new destinations where they are shared to create a sense of belonging and to recall a homeland that has been left. At the same time, traditional recipes are transformed and adapted to include new ingredients and tastes. Finally, food becomes the currency through which new connections are made and a way to introduce traditions to a new home country.

While the cultural dimensions of transnationalism are critical to migration, a great deal of the research on the topic focuses only on economics. At its most basic, transnational economics serve to tie sending and destination communities together through the pull of markets and the remittances that follow. The strong social and cultural attachments that characterize most migrants allow the efforts of the individual mover to reach beyond his immediate needs to include his family and even community. In other words, the migrant must succeed to secure not just her own well-being, but that of her family, sending household, and community. Typically this is accomplished through remittances. Literally billions of dollars are flowing around the globe as migrants send money home (Acosta et al. 2006; Cohen 2005). In places as diverse as Turkey, Brazil, El Salvador, and the Philippines migrants are celebrated as national heroes whose efforts and remittances are often the largest source of capital available to their country. Yet remittances do not serve the same purposes for everyone; as funds flow to sending countries and regions, households use the income in different ways.

Working in southern Mexico, Cohen noted that all households, regardless of what their migrant member was doing, earmarked some remitted funds to cover the costs of everyday life; in the state of Oaxaca nearly 80 percent of the households with migrants depended on remittances to cover nearly all expenses. In other situations, remittances might go to investment (Ratha 2007). Other things are remitted as well, and Smith (2006) notes that migrants often organize in their destination communities to support the growth of their hometowns. Typically, migrants organize HTAs (hometown associations) to collect funds from co-migrants and their descendents to cover big-ticket items. A favorite among Mexican migrants to the U.S. is the purchase of an ambulance for a sending community. Usually, migrants meet and organize and decide how much each member should contribute. They may also plan a fund-raiser around an event. The outcome may take some time, but the money is collected and an ambulance is purchased and driven to the sending community. In the sending community, the ambulance provides transportation to regional hospitals (health care in rural Mexico is spotty at best, and hospitals are often located in urban centers; rural folk have a hard time accessing care). While the effort is appreciated, such remittances can cause problems; once in Mexico, ambulances sent from the U.S. often are unmanned and slowly fail as trained paramedics and drivers are hard to find and the salaries of such individuals as well as the maintenance of the vehicles are often beyond the means of a community.

Political activism creates a third kind of transnational space for migrants and their communities. Political activism develops as migrants gain voices through which they are able to critique their sending nations and its policies. Often migrants are critical of state leaders and their goals. Because they are in a foreign country and generally free of internal forms of harassment and persecution, they are able to develop a critical voice. They are able to organize and protest corruption, mistreatment, and broken promises from a secure position. They can also create room for change, and many migrant groups have played instrumental roles as their sending states acknowledge their importance and court their support. This often leads to migrants and expatriates gaining the right to vote in sending nation elections. Political activists also use their status in foreign countries to uncover and expose the excesses of the leaders in their sending countries. This can mean exposing corruption or disclosing how the state meddles in local affairs.

Refugees often become politically engaged in the affairs of their sending countries in ways they could not as citizens. The opportunities to critique the leaders of their nations from the security of a destination country allow them to gain a voice in the political affairs of their sending nation and to foment change, or at least create the opportunity for change. Various Middle Eastern examples illustrate this, such as Turkish Kurds' political mobilizations in Germany and other European countries and Iranians' demonstrations in European capitals. The Kurdistan Workers Party (the

PKK) has been very strong in Europe and organized mass demonstrations against the possible imposition of the death penalty on their leader Abdullah Ocalan in 1999 and 2000.[10] While the ability of migrant groups to effect change in their origin countries is unproven, the very fact that migrants gain a voice in debates is a sign of the important role such political activism plays. In later chapters we will discuss this as one aspect of the remittance debate concerning nonfinancial benefits to the sending society.

Finally, transnational social ties are critical to the migrant. Transnational social ties are practical as well as symbolic. Most international migrants in the contemporary world depend upon transnational social networks to maneuver across national borders. The social ties to migrants already established in their destination communities as well as to sending families are critical to success. Migrants depend upon social ties to sending families to support what can be expensive moves. Turning to a family for support can mean a migrant does not need to ask a smuggler for assistance. He does not have to go into debt (or perhaps can go into less debt) to cover the expenses of a border crossing. Migrants also depend upon established migrants in their destination who have already worked through border crossings. They turn to these individuals for advice on routes as well as aid in settling, finding a job, and finding friends. While such ties can at times be a hindrance (migrants who depend too much on social ties tend to find less diverse opportunities and are sometimes limited in their choices because of community pressures once they have settled), social networks offer supports that often ease the insecurity that migrants encounter in their moves.

Transnational social networks also keep migrants connected to their sending communities over time and space (Rios 2008). It is not unusual for the children and grandchildren of migrants to maintain ties to distant and seldom-visited sending communities. These connections are motivated and maintained through transnational linkages. The linkages define identity and embed the migrant in a social universe that is organized around sending household and family, community, and ethnic group. This is clear in the actions of Mixtecos who migrate to the U.S. and the second and third generation of children who are the descendents of those early migrants. The children of Mixteco migrants keep their language alive and they are tied to sending communities they have never visited. More importantly, they continue to remit to those communities. A similar pattern is followed by Somali refugees, who continue to support families in Somalia as well as refugee camps in Kenya (Valentine, Sporton, and Nielsen 2009).

CONCLUSIONS

International migration involves millions of people moving about the globe. And while many of these people are looking for new opportunities and trying to escape the restrictions of their sending homes, towns, and countries, an amazing number of migrants continue to rely upon and support those nations long after they have departed. We have captured some of this quality in our discussion of transnationalism and the outcomes of international migration.

International migration is just another kind of mobility and, like internal mobility, it is motivated by a number of reasons and in response to a range of possibilities and limits. It is also important to understand that while international migration is critical for many people in our world who rely upon remittances to support themselves, the movers are not to blame for outcomes. In other words, blaming migrants for the problems that face a receiving nation is not the answer; such an attitude avoids placing the burden on the governments of nations whose decisions motivate migration. It also avoids placing blame on destination countries that turn a blind eye to migration as they seek a low-wage and cheap labor force that will not complain while publicly objecting to the very migrants they attract. We are reminded of the scene in *Casablanca* when the police chief complains, "I cannot believe there is gambling taking place in this establishment," just as he is given his winnings for the night.

Five

NONMOVERS AND THOSE
WHO STAY BEHIND

If I had had to ask somebody— "can I stay back?"—at that
moment, I would have been gone. Why should I ask somebody
to be able to stay back in [my] own home?
—DR. VIMLA DHAR, A KASHMIRI PANDIT DOCTOR

We noted that mobility includes movers who follow local
commutes, migrants who travel to internal destinations, and migrants who
cross borders and are bound for international destinations. The numbers
of movers involved is staggeringly big. There are literally millions of individuals who are involved in migration in one way or another. Some move
on their own volition while others are forced to travel. Some are looking for jobs and relatively higher wages, others—particularly refugees—
are looking for a safe place to settle, while some others could be going in
search of an adventure, a pilgrimage, an education, or self-actualization.
Nevertheless, citing the overwhelming numbers of movers around the
world does not fully communicate what is happening. In fact, in the nineteenth and early twentieth centuries, migrants formed a larger percentage
of the global population than they do today. Furthermore, while we may
know that one migrant is a refugee while another is looking for a job, the
dynamics between movers and those who stay behind is often obscured.

It might seem odd, but we need to remember that billions of people
around the world never migrate. They are called "nonmigrants," "nonmovers," "stay-at-homes," and "immobile social actors." Yet they are central
to the migration process and outcomes, and they are indirectly and directly
affected by mobility and the outcomes of movement. Nonmovers play a
key role for migrants as they are traveling the globe (Hammar and Tamas
1997). Nonmigrants are critically important as foci for action and interest
to migrants and to the states and nations migrants leave. Nonmigrants are
anchors for migrants, they are a pool of potential movers for the future,

and they are the members of households who depend upon the remittances of their migrant members to survive. They are more as well, for while they may be nonmigrants and immobile, they are not free of the social burdens and cultural pressures that can be linked to migration. They are central in discussions of identity and in debates concerning native, local, rural, or indigenous society in the modern world. They are also a focus of the debates surrounding integration and citizenship and are often at the center of disputes between movers and their states.

In this chapter we focus on nonmovers and show that they are critical to understanding mobility and the cultural, social, and economic impact of migration.

NONMIGRANTS

In a way, everyone who is not involved in moving is a nonmigrant or a nonmover. If you live where you were born, you are a "stay-at-home." Of course, using the title "nonmovers" to describe people in sending households and countries does not help in the discussion of movement and migration as it assumes immobility and a stillness that often belies the active role people who do not migrate often play. We will focus instead on the relationship of movers and nonmovers and think about nonmigrants and stay-at-homes as those people who are members of migrant households but not the movers.[1]

The nonmigrating members of the migrant households are critical social actors in the migration process. For many migrants, stay-at-homes are the connection that anchors and secures the migrant as he or she moves. However, it is not just anchoring but also a facilitating function we need to discern here. Within the household, those left behind are not disadvantaged; they are facilitating actors in the process of migration. Nonmigrants are often central to the migration decision. And of course, remittances flow from migrants to nonmigrants. As we have already discussed, migrants do not typically remit to communities—rather they send funds to families that are left behind in the migration process (Cohen 2002). Those families may use remitted funds to cover community expenses, but these payments are usually made in the name of the migrant or family and are not donated anonymously to a village. Even the migrants who forsake their families—in other words, those migrants who do not remit—impact the lives of nonmovers. Recent work shows that nonmovers are suffering as remittances by migrants decline globally (Ratha and Mohapatra 2009).

Mexican migrants find themselves not earning as much as in the past and so they cannot send as much money home; in turn, nonmigrants in origin communities suffer, reduce the money they spend, and go without both luxuries and critical commodities as budgets get tight (Vivar 2009). Finally, nonmigrants might be refugees who cannot afford to leave the camps where they live. Perhaps some family members, relatives, or co-ethnics do find the opportunity to migrate, but many cannot exit their camps or cross borders of any kind.

In many settings we find that there is a progression in the migration process; and at each stage, there are stay-at-homes. Early movers are married men who have some resources and can afford to travel. Their sojourns are personal but also made in the effort to support a family and children. As men age and their children grow, their young, unmarried sons will often take their places and travel to a destination community and in the process support their families and begin to learn new skills. As children age and establish their own families and households their migration decisions change. With a household to manage and young children to raise the decision to migrate is made not in relation to what parents want or need, but in terms of the demands of the new household. A newly established household likely has debts to repay. When young children appear, new stresses also arise. Children must be educated and cared for and where opportunities are limited, migration may be the only real option. Finally as individuals age and if they are migrants living far from their sending households, they may elect to return home and retire. Even death can be an issue for movers and nonmovers as the deceased are repatriated to their origin families and communities.

The role of the nonmovers is different where migration is a rite of passage (Rouse 1991). Young men often mark their growth and pending adulthood through migration, and those moves do not stand apart but engage the community and household (see Chap. 6 in Monto 1994). The mover relies on nonmovers and their community to organize and bring meaning to the rite. The nonmovers are also engaged to help cover the expenses of the rite. Finally, the sending household and community are there when the mover is ready to return.

Nonmigrants are regularly involved in migration discussions. When a migrant leaves a household and community, they are not really free to travel and make independent decisions. Stay-at-homes influence a migrant's overall decisions on destination as well as employment. For example, among Filipinos, parents will often push their children toward the U.S. and nursing as a career. They know it is a safe, well-established, and

lucrative avenue to success (Semyonov and Gorodzeisky 2005). The decision to support a child's migration begins long before a move can take place
as parents enroll their children in nursing schools. They pool resources to
cover expenses, paperwork, and transportation. In return, a child may feel
rather limited and controlled. Of course, some children cannot complete a
program, others drop out, and still others will simply leave a program and
turn away from their families. Yet even migrants who turn their backs on
their sending households are leaving family behind, and often that family
must struggle to cover the loss. The loss is exacerbated where the migrant
leaves behind young children, who grow older not really knowing a parent (Hagan, Eschbach, and Rodriguez 2008; Heymann et al. 2009; Ryan
et al. 2009). Generally, one outcome of migration is to enhance the status
and health of the children left behind, yet when both parents migrate and
a child is fostered with grandparents, other relatives, or friends, the outcomes are ambiguous; while the situation may not cost the child in terms
of health outcomes, it does rob her of critical social relationships.

   We noted above that age is a critical factor in determining who will be
nonmigrants. As individuals grow older, they are less likely to migrate; and
of course the very young lack skills, cannot work, and also do not wish
to enter the migrant stream. Gender also has a bearing on migration outcomes; in many traditional settings it is more difficult for women to cross
borders, although that is changing. Nevertheless, it isn't without reason
that people joke that most rural communities are now a unique mixture
of nurseries and senior centers as young and able-bodied adults have left.
In some settings women are now the majority of movers. Yet the numbers
are somewhat misleading. In the past, women watched as their fathers,
brothers, and husbands left to cross borders. Now that most of the men
who can leave as migrants have migrated, more women are crossing borders as well.

   Nonmovers are, of course, deeply concerned with migration outcomes.
They do not want to look on as members of the household leave and do
not remit or maintain contact. Instead, nonmovers want migrants to remain engaged with their sending community and households. They use all
of their skills to keep the migrant engaged. They may ask the migrant to
serve in local government. Alternatively, they may ask the migrant to support a celebration, ritual, or cultural event that requires money and leadership. Sometimes this works well enough to encourage the migrant to return to his or her sending community. In San Francisco Cajonos, Oaxaca,
Mexico, the village's *presidente municipal* (something more-or-less like a
mayor) in 2004 was a gentleman who had spent decades in the U.S., was a

naturalized citizen, and had most of his family living in San Diego, California. Yet he always contributed to his sending community, supporting his parents and other relatives who did not leave the village. When he was asked to return to the village and serve, he did so because he felt obligated. The obligation was not extreme, only a year, and he returned to finish what he calls a "vacation home" in the village and reestablish his social status vis-à-vis the small group of San Franciscans who continued to call the community home (Sanchez 2007).

People at home regularly ask for remittances to support family. They may plan a business with the migrant and ask him to send specific resources home. Nevertheless, the majority of money remitted, and in particular remittances to rural households, goes to family support. In other words, remittances go to covering food, clothing, and daily expenses. Such an arrangement can be problematic. Migrants often voice their disappointment that the money they send home is not supporting investments. Stay-at-homes sometimes fear that they are "misusing" what is remitted as so much goes to daily expenses. The point here is not that one kind of remittance practice is good and another is bad—rather, it is that the migration process is stressful for the nonmigrant as well as the migrant. Nonmigrants are under pressure to cover for a household's missing members. When women are left behind, they often find themselves in new positions vis-à-vis the migrants who have left. Their roles, which were largely domestic in the past, now include managing money and finding work to support all of the household's members who are not migrating. Finally, there is a great deal of stress for stay-at-homes. As the costs of migration increase and tensions on most international borders rise, it isn't unusual to encounter nonmigrants who are under a great deal of stress and must cope with those stresses, raise children alone, manage a household, and organize a budget on their own.

NONMOVERS AS FUTURE MIGRANTS

A nonmover is not destined to remain immobile over time. In fact, nonmigrants and stay-at-homes are only defined as immobile because when we meet them, they are not involved in the migration process. Perhaps they were migrants and have elected to stay home. Such folks were migrants in the past, just not at the moment. To describe them as immobile is to overlook the migrations they once experienced. Furthermore, because migration is a cumulative process, or one that builds upon itself over time, the experiences of migrants and nonmigrants are integral to the actions of contemporary, present-day migrants. Thus, we talk to non-movers and stay-at-homes to get their views of migration, their opinions on their own dependence on remittances, and their ideas concerning the future of mobility.

Nonmigrants in households exercise a great deal of influence over migrants. Together, nonmovers and potential movers decide on destinations. If a potential migrant is a young man without a family, perhaps he will be sent overseas. If he is a young man with a family, the migration decision likely rests in the discussion he will have with both his parents and his spouse. Young women will more than likely be encouraged not to cross an international border or to seek work that is tied to the household (as a maid, for example) and living arrangements with relatives (a brother or father). Nonmigrants also depend on migrants for support. Across the globe remittances, as we have noted, are critical to survival. Nonmovers typically rely on remittances to cover the costs of daily life and make up for local wage work that is limited in availability and pays very little.

It is the case for many nonmovers that someone in their family has already departed for a domestic or international destination. For others migration is simply not possible. The costs of moving to a domestic or international destination are just too high or perhaps the nonmover has work that renders migration a costly and questionable possibility. Some non-movers may doubt the value of migration, and their immobility is a critical statement on their opinion of the value of migration. Other nonmovers make a conscious decision to stay in their communities of origin.

While some decisions concerning immobility are based in assumptions about the value of the hometown as an ideal place to exercise cultural identity with little or no disputes, many nonmovers are making choices about their futures that give little regard to immediate issues of security and insecurity. Like the migrants they send to domestic and international destinations, nonmovers create, re-create, and challenge the construction and meaning of social identities and transnational social spaces. They stay put and challenge removal; they undermine forced migrations and in so doing they ensure that past and place are not abandoned but instead remain integral to the definition of identity and belonging.

Nonmovers are anchors for both migrants and other nonmovers. Non-migrants create identity in their interpretations of new practices and traditions as well as their use of those very practices and traditions. At a basic level, new practices brought by returning migrants are given a local interpretation and made to hold value according to traditional practices. In other words, nonmigrants take the cultural and social artifacts that are sent home (or that come home with returning migrants) and make them their own. Flea markets in the South Pacific island nation of Tonga are an ideal example of this process (Brown and Connell 1994). Brown and Connell note that Tongan flea markets combine traditional economic practices and a growing reliance on international remittances. Nonmigrants who receive remittances use those funds to support the creation of a new market system and, acting as entrepreneurs, fortify the local domestic economy, which is organized around agriculture and limited craft production. Tongan entrepreneurs anchor identity through their relationships with migrants and other nonmovers, creating "transnational kin corporations" that transcend space and bridge differences in local economic practices (Brown and Connell 1994:640).

Migrants rely upon nonmovers for their physical well-being as well as social support as they cross borders, find work, and settle. Households generally support the migrations of their members, often by covering the expenses of migration and sometimes by sacrifice. In many situations, nonmovers organize the funds necessary to cross a border. They may ask for support from friends and family, but generally the goal is to organize the resources to cover a migration without going into debt or taking a loan. Cohen found that families covered nearly three-quarters of the costs of most migrations to the U.S. (2004). Of course, the nonmigrants expect the migrant to remit as a way to repay the family. Sometimes there still is not enough money, and a nonmigrant must make sacrifices to cover the costs of border crossing. The nonmigrant may have to give up her own dream of border crossing. At other points, the nonmigrant will take work he might not want, perhaps dropping out of school or a training program, to help a family cope with the loss of a migrant who has not yet begun to remit funds home.

MIGRANTS AS FUTURE NONMOVERS

Just as nonmovers can become migrants, migrants do become nonmovers. Migrants who settle in new destinations also look to nonmovers as they create a sense of their own identity. In their new settings they reproduce and react to the traditions and practices they know and believe to be critical to their origin community. Thus nonmovers are not only adapting to the changes they encounter in their new destinations, but defining and redefining identities in relation to origin communities as well as destinations. Often the process is one where traditional practices, symbols, and relationships that are critical to an origin community are transposed and reinvented in a destination.

Another issue when we talk about immobility concerns migrants who are living in a destination community. Some of these individuals settled in their new communities with no interest in returning to their sending villages; in respect to cases like these we must ask how long it takes for a migrant to become a nonmover in a new setting. Our discussions of settled migrants often focus on "children of migrants," or "second-generation migrants." We would argue that such a label marks mobility as something like an identifier of ethnicity or identity. Sometimes, as in the case of Turks in Germany, Mexicans in the U.S., and Pakistanis in England, it is difficult for the children of migrants to escape the link between ethnicity and mobility. In the case of each of these groups, there is a strong association between ethnicity and the original migrant population. This connection can restrict opportunities regardless of a migrant's background and ability.[2] One response is for migrants and their children to seek new communities where they are not recognized as members of minority migrant populations. Such a process has played out as Mexican immigrants move to the U.S. Midwest (Millard and Chapa 2004), where they do not face the discrimination they often encounter in more traditional destinations like southern California or Texas (Menchaca 1995). Some migrants effectively distance themselves from co-ethnic movers to settle and create new communities around shared common practices with others to facilitate their integration (Vaiou and Stratigaki 2008). Other migrants settle in their new communities, yet keep strong ties with their sending households and communities.

Migrants who settle in new destination communities often find themselves involved in politics. However, unlike native-born citizens, migrants are involved in the politics not only of their new nation, but sometimes — and more importantly — of their sending nation and community. Migrants to new destinations often find they are able to assess and criticize their home nation in ways that were impossible from the perspective of an origin household. Sometimes the new destination offers migrants a voice as they earn a living and become participants in the life of the new nation. Other times the distance from a sending country and the protections of a destination country's laws allow for criticism. Co-ethnics also find that as they come together because of their shared background, they can establish strong and critical identities that, as we noted above, build from traditional relationships to negotiate new avenues and outcomes. This is clear among Mixtecos (Indians from southern Mexico), who have organized in the

U.S. first to create a sense of shared identity and second to use that identity to critique the Mexican state (Rivera-Salgado 1999; Rivera-Salgado and Rabandan 2004). A sense of identity comes not simply from living together in a new destination, but from rebuilding a sense of identity with and belonging to a defined group through shared language, celebrations, and even the use of leisure time; in the case of Mixtecos, this means playing basketball in the U.S., but on teams that are dedicated to sending communities in Mexico. It also means broadcasting in native languages. Finally, the efforts of the Mixtecos reach well beyond the local community and form a strong voice criticizing the actions of the Mexican state generally—regarding broadly defined agricultural and neoliberal policies—but also specifically—as when the governor in Oaxaca gave a strong-armed, violent response to local demonstrators protesting his policies (see Cohen 2007 for discussion of these events). Pakistanis, Iranians, Kurds, and Turks who have settled in various parts of Europe—and will likely never return to their sending communities and households—have also organized efforts to critique their respective native states.

Sirkeci (2006a:265–272), in his research in Germany, noted that even as first-generation Turkish and Kurdish immigrants settled in Germany, they continued to mourn the loss of their homeland over time. They had children who were born in Germany (i.e., second generation), where they grew up, got married, and gave birth to grandsons and granddaughters (i.e., third generation). These relationships tied the first-generation migrants to that new "home" country. Some of them happily settled, while some others felt trapped but also chose to stay (2006a:272). After spending three decades or more as guest-workers in Germany, some sadly realized that their friends who remained in Turkey had passed away, and they then felt there was no reason to return. In many cases, second and third generations are not moving back to their ancestral home countries. Nevertheless, the second- and third-generation children and grandchildren of immigrants are often treated as immigrants themselves. In other words, they became nonmovers, but they did not fully assimilate into German society as might be expected. Rather, Turks in Germany, Poles and Pakistanis in England, and Mexicans in the U.S. are examples of "segmentary assimilation" and the social and economic downward mobility of movers as they settle in destination countries (Waldinger and Lichter 2003). Their assimilation does not follow a "traditional" path and they do not become equal citizens. Instead, they find that they are consigned to ethnic enclaves and low-skilled jobs that limit their engagement with their destination countries and societies.

Immigrants and later generations form various kinds of organizations with political, economic, religious, or cultural purposes. Some argue that such organizations help their integration with the host society (Freedman 2004; Gonzalez 2009; Pantoja 2005) while others emphasize their critical role in creating transnational communities (Nell 2004). However, native-born citizens also perceive immigrant communities and the descendents of immigrants as largely defined by a home country. Many of the Muslim Asians protesting against the returning British troops from Afghanistan were British born. The chants of "Go home" by the soldiers were quite ambiguous given the birthplace of the majority of the protestors, and suggests just how difficult it is to separate the immigrant from the local.

CONCLUSIONS

It is easy to omit nonmigrants from our discussions of mobility. Our studies are focused on movers, and when it comes to policy issues, nonmovers and stay-at-homes are not part of the problem. For many policy makers the problem is how to get fewer people to migrate. We have argued that we need to look at both movers and nonmovers to make sense of mobility; if we focus only on movers we cannot fully understand the connections that link migrants and stay-at-homes. Migration is a strategy that builds upon mobility not by asking everyone to migrate but by creating opportunities for origin households to organize and survive over time through the inclusion of migration in internal decision making.

Six

THE ECONOMICS OF MIGRATION
AND THE POSSIBILITIES OF
DEVELOPMENT

*Remittances can help reduce poverty of recipient households
and, perhaps, some other households in the neighborhood. But
remittances cannot be a substitute for growth and employment
generation efforts at home.*
— DILIP RATHA, IN A 2009 INTERVIEW

*Every Dominican who lives abroad is expected to send home
remittances. Most Dominicans, in the States [U.S.] at least, are
intending to return here for their retirement. They send home
money to help their families and their communities. I even had
some of them in New York who asked me if I wanted them to
send money to me when I returned.*
— LETTY GUTIERREZ, INTERVIEWED AFTER
RETURNING TO THE DOMINICAN REPUBLIC

Migrant remittances are the resources that migrants return
to their sending households. Remittances flow to sending households from
both internal movers and international sojourners and take many forms.
Most discussions of remittance practices focus on money that flows from
the migrants in their destination communities to their families living in
sending households (OECD 2005). The total amount of remittances that
flowed to developing countries was estimated to be $72 billion in 2002,
which was much higher than total official aid directed to the developing
world (COE 2006:7). Reports like the OECD's review of global remittance
practices noted that two years later (2004) the total returned by migrants
increased to at least $126 billion (OECD 2005). Furthermore, these trace-
able dollars do not include informal transfers, which may double the value
of remittances (ibid.). It is no surprise that remittances are likely the second largest source of external capital (following only foreign direct invest-

ment) for most developing countries. Remittances generate much-needed foreign currency to recipient countries as well as supporting millions of poor families across the world.

The value of the dollars flowing around the globe is quite amazing; yet remittances usually include more than money. Migrants often send goods to their homes and families that range from big-ticket items (such as ambulances, fire trucks, and autobuses; see Smith 2006) to small gifts that are irregularly returned (Cliggett 2005). Regardless of the size or quality of the remittance, what migrants send home is important.

Remittances are a sign of the continued involvement of the migrant in the life of his or her sending household and by extension the community. Remittances support the families that migrants leave behind and in particular the children, who cannot travel (Rose and Shaw 2008). Remittances carry information between movers and nonmovers and create linkages and reinforce responsibilities that can reach beyond the original mover and include her children and grandchildren (Moran-Taylor 2008) or influence marriage decisions and outcomes (Ali 2007). Remittances also reach beyond sending households to aid family and friends, including individuals who share lineal or tribal identities and communities (Voigt-Graf 2008). Finally, remittances bring changes for movers as well as those left behind. The money, goods, and resources that a migrant returns both drive and satisfy the costs associated with new demands, new ideas, and new ways of life (Conway 2007; Conway and Potter 2007).[1]

The shifts that remittances bring are obvious in the goods nonmigrants demand (often including small domestic items, computers, televisions, and the like). New foods, new ways of eating and cooking, and new ways of talking about traditional practices also travel home with migrants and remittances. In fact, some nonmigrants will abandon traditional practices, including agriculture, as they learn new value systems and as global changes as well as national laws (such as new land regulations in Mexico) refocus how people think about work and society (Wilk 2006). Where subsistence agriculture was the norm, nonmigrants often combine limited wage work with a growing reliance on remittances, turning away from traditional practices.

While the importance and influence of remittances are clear, there is an intense debate over the role of remittances as tools for generalized economic development. In this chapter we focus on remittances, define their flow and meaning, and examine their debated role in development. We also shift the discussion from a focus chiefly on remittances to consider issues of security and insecurity and argue that it is the search for security as well as an escape from insecurity that can drive mobility and frame remittance practices. Finally, we explore the response of destination countries to the remittance practices of the migrants who have come to live in them. We argue that a negative response—in other words, the assumption that migrants are a burden and cost to a destination country—may miss the important investments that migrants make.

REMITTANCES AND DEVELOPMENT

Anything a migrant sends to her or his sending home is a remittance. And while discussions of remittances tend to focus on the large transfers of money that come from international movers (World Bank 2006), we must recognize the various ways in which migrants organize remittances.

Migrants do not simply deliver remittances to their sending households. Rather, remittances are something that migrants return only after they have settled in their new destinations. Migrants have to find housing and jobs and they are likely faced with bills and costs that limit their ability to remit over the early portion of their resettlements. In chapters 3 and 4 we noted that internal and international migrants tend to settle with family and friends and that they rely upon family and friends to find work. If a migrant is able to acquire a place to live and if he or she is able to find work quickly, they may begin remitting with little delay. However, many contemporary migrants, and particularly international movers, first have to pay for the expense of their border crossing and they may owe thousands of dollars to smugglers; the first months or years of their sojourns are likely focused on paying these costs (Andrade-Eekhoff 2006; Nangengast, Stavenhagen, and Kearney 1992; Runsten and Kearney 1994).[2]

Once immediate expenses are covered, and housing and a job are found, a migrant may begin to remit. Yet even the settled migrant must first organize his or her income to cover expenses. In response, initial remittances made by migrants to sending households are often quite small as the migrant is settling in. A migrant has to deal with rent, utilities, food, entertainment, and the like; all of these expenses, whether they are legitimate or not, are a burden on incomes. Often migrants will live together in small apartment units in rather marginal parts of a community to cut expenses. Most movers, internal as well as international, find work in agriculture, service, and construction. Agricultural jobs range from working on farms for set wages and following national labor agreement programs—such as the Bracero program in the U.S., which ran from 1942 to 1962, and current programs in Canada that bring Latin Americans (mostly Mexicans) to jobs on farms. There are of course many more migrants who find agricultural work that is not formally recognized (Chavez 1994; Miera 2008; Schwartzman 2009).

Throughout the world, service work ranges from formal labor in small stores and businesses to informal day labor (packing and unpacking moving boxes, for example) and domestic work (Haney 1979; Hondagneu-Sotelo 1994; Kinoti 2006; Vandegrift 2008). The demand for unskilled labor and the shift toward service work is a mark of contemporary migration and a significant change from the past, when migration was driven by the need for industrial labor. Even construction work, a kind of labor that demands some background training and strength, is managed nowadays largely as if it were a service. Contractors hire migrants to join crews, but often the migrant works with falsely created documents "off the books" (Blank, Danziger, and Schoeni 2006; Zlolniski 2006).

While the wages migrants earn may seem very high when compared with the wages available in most sending countries,[3] migrants often take multiple jobs to earn more and over a shorter period of time. Skill and experience also contribute to increased wages as does the ability to speak the dominant language of the destination country. Regardless of incomes and ability of the migrant, it is estimated that anywhere from 60 to 80 percent of the wages earned by migrants go to immediate expenses in the destination country and are not remitted (Bean et al. 1998; Duleep and Dowhan 2008; Stark and Taylor 1989).[4] In England a similar pattern exists, as migrant earnings also flow into governmental programs. For example, the United Kingdom National Health Service is dependent on overseas doctors and nurses, who constitute a majority of the medical staff in many hospitals across the country. This is the reason they can afford to have a Polish doctor flying in every other week to treat Scottish patients.

Private-sector banks also earn a great deal from the efforts of migrants. Borjas (2003) analyzed the earnings of immigrants over decades and estimated that the potential surplus created by immigrants in the U.S. ranged from $8.4 billion to $70 billion per annum (Borjas 1999). Moses and Letnes (2003:12) criticize this work and argue that Borjas underestimates the volume of the surplus. And while Borjas estimates about $400 per head per annum, Moses and Letnes argue, "The richest countries tend to benefit by about US$ 3,600 per migrant per year, whereas the middle-income and poorest countries tend to lose" from about $1,000 to $2,700 (Moses and Letnes 2003:12–13).[5] Although many immigrants close the earning gap with natives in the long run, often they never draw even, earning up to 30 percent less than their native peers even ten years after their arrival in the U.S. (Borjas 2003:4).

REMITTANCES

While it is hard to track internal migrants and the remittances they send, generally we can assume their remittances to be small in comparison to international transfers (Borjas 2006). In Mexico, remittances by internal migrants were about one-sixth the size of those returned by international migrants (see Cohen 2004). Many migrants who do not cross national borders often remit very little. Working with Zambian migrants, Cliggett found that the remittances returned by rural-to-urban migrants as well as movers traveling to other sub-Saharan African countries were trivial in size (2005). Generally, movers returned what sending households considered gifts—small amounts of money or simple presents (toys, clothes, and small appliances) that were inexpensive. These gifts traveled home infrequently and did not help to support a family, cover daily expenses, or encourage any kind of saving or investment. Nevertheless, the gifts helped migrants maintain ties with their sending households and by extension communities and were linkages that were used to support movement, resettlement, and job seeking. In other words, the migrants used remittances, even though they were small, to strengthen and maintain ties to home.[6]

Remittances from international movers range from the small gifts sent infrequently that we noted above to large regular monthly or bimonthly payments that are returned to sending households and support everyday life, schooling, rituals, and healthcare as well as investments and economic growth. These remittances are crucial, particularly to rural folk, who do not have opportunities to find work or for those households and communities that lack infrastructures to create work opportunities.

Where natural disasters have struck, remittances are often critical to the very survival of a local population. Working in Haiti, Fagen (2006) notes that the efforts of migrants in Canada, the U.S., and Europe were central to the survival and recovery of the country and its populace following tropical storm Jeanne in September 2004. The storm devastated Haiti, killing thousands and flooding the nation's third-largest city. The response by Western nations was critical and rapid and aided the government in its immediate response to the destruction, yet it was the efforts of Haitians living in North America and Europe that led to the rebuilding of Gonaives as well as other smaller villages affected by the storm. Haitian migrants remitted millions of dollars, but also goods (ranging from food to clothing to appliances) to support rebuilding. In the process there was created "a 'chain of solidarity' among neighbors, relatives still in the country, international humanitarian agencies that came to the city to help, and overseas relatives" (Fagen 2006:15). And while Fagen notes that the efforts of Haitians living abroad were central to rebuilding efforts, the remittances returned did not alleviate poverty, lead to formal changes in government, or encourage governmental participation. In fact, she notes that few Haitians at home or abroad expect much from the central government.[7]

The example of Haiti highlights the role remittances play in moments of crisis, yet remittances are critical on a daily basis for many people. Many rural households have come to depend on remittances to cover a significant part of their daily expenses. These are not households that expect the occasional gift of little real economic value; rather, they count on migrants and the funds they remit to cover a large portion and often the majority of the expenses they face. Rural households in Mexico, Morocco, Haiti, and other countries meet 20–60 percent of their expenses through the remittances returned by migrants (Adams 1989; Adams and Page 2005; Hernandez and Coutin 2006; Kinoti 2006; Lozano Ascencio 1993; Portes and Guarnizo 1991; Skeldon 2008; Taylor and Wyatt 1996). These funds go to cover immediate expenses like food, clothing, and utilities, but also costs that are associated with ritual and community such as saint's day celebrations or village political hierarchies (see Cohen 2004). At the same time, remittances support individuals as they move away from traditional agriculture and abandon their fields; while these processes are most clearly understood for Mexico, they are not restricted to North America but in fact occur globally (Brumer 2008; Cordell 1996; Manning 2002; Martin 2002; Todaro 1996).

The use of remittances follows the development, demands, and needs of a household. Young, newly established families tend to earmark their remittances to cover daily expenses and home improvements that can range from bringing in utilities to finishing rooms, improving kitchens and bathrooms, and the like. Young families also earmark remittances to help cover schooling for children. Sometimes money goes to ritual expenses that the young couple incurred around their marriage and birth of young children. This is the case in rural Mexico, where migrants earmark remittances to help repay reciprocal loans that are made for a wedding and birth of children (Cohen 2004).

Older families typically have a well-appointed home to live in and may be able to use some of their remittances for new social expenses, such as making loans to younger migrants and supporting younger couples. At the same time, education may be more expensive as young children grow older and enter colleges and technical training programs. Growing children also place new demands on a household and ask for new goods and services, including cellular telephones, computers, and even vehicles.

Households with international movers are sometimes able to earmark remittances for investment. Often expenses at home have declined, children are grown, and home improvements are completed. Now remittances can be directed toward business growth. Working in rural Morocco, de Haas (2006a:571) has shown that remittances from international movers enhance households' statuses but also create a "new major socio-economic divide" that transcends ethnicity and establishes divisions that supersede traditional status differences. He finds this is particularly true among *ismakhen* (ex-slaves) and *haratin* (landless or smallholding serfs and sharecroppers); and the "black" oasis population who are subordinate to the "white" *imazighen*, who possess land and water resources. Households that receive remittances from international movers, regardless of their ethnicity, are more likely to purchase land, invest in pumps and dairy production, and grow a larger variety of crops that can be sold on the local market. Styan (2007) moves beyond Morocco and argues that the patterns found there are paralleled throughout much of Africa, where remittances from international movers become critical tools in stable economic growth. Beyond the positive impact that remittances have for households, Styan also notes that many countries are following the lead of Mexico, Brazil, Turkey, and the Philippines to develop state programs that leverage remittances and support increased national development.

National governments are not immune to the growing sense that international remittances can drive economic growth. Several countries, including Brazil, El Salvador, and Turkey, now describe migrants as "heroes" whose efforts support the growth of GNP and enhance the balance of trade. This is clearly the case in El Salvador, where remittances are overwhelmingly the most important source of foreign capital for the nation (Andrade-Eekhoff 2006). Even in countries with strong traditions of industry, natural resources, and international trade, remittances are growing in importance. In Mexico, remittances are one of the top sources of foreign capital for the nation and are second only to petroleum as a national resource—which may be a surprise for a country with a rich history of industrial production. The OECD (2005) notes that economic growth follows several pathways among migrant-sending countries. National governments create programs that match remittances and create opportunities for expanded growth, such as Mexico's *Tres-por-Uno* (three-for-one) program, in which communities that petition the federal government and are approved receive three pesos from the government for each peso invested and typically these monies come as remittances from individual migrants (Fernández de Castro et al. 2006; Staffon et al. 2006).[8] A second set consists of programs defined by migrants that focus on local growth, with the hopes of pulling the state into a more active role. Finally, a third set of programs develops around nongovernmental agencies that promote growth through partnering programs that link migrant-sending regions with foreign-funded training and development programs that encourage growth (Fox 2007; Martin, Midgley, and Teitelbaum 2002; Portes 2007; Taylor et al. 1996).

While the role of remittances in development is clear in these examples, many researchers express serious reservations when it comes to the role remittances play in inspiring migration (Adams 1996; Bovenkerk 1982; Rubenstein 1982). First, there are the costs associated with migration. As we noted above, a large portion of the money earned by migrants remains in their destination country or region and cannot be remitted. Furthermore, migrants are paid wages that cannot compete with those paid to native workers. The combination, it is argued, makes remittances an inefficient source of income for a sending household (for example, see Binford 2003). In other words, the migrant earns little and uses a great deal of what he or she earns just paying for the costs of living in the destination community. Remittances suffer in response, with little money actually destined for rural households. Furthermore, the experience of migration and the growth of border crossing as a viable option that can reduce work efforts and traditional labor practices in sending countries is creating what is often described as a "syndrome" that is not only self-perpetuating, but also potentially destructive of traditional cultural practices (Mittelman 2000; Reichert 1981).

A second problem arises around what some researchers see as the declining value of the nation-state as a force in internal growth and development and in the rising importance of remittances to local communities. While the OECD and the World Bank trumpet the important role migrant remittances play, there is a growing body of evidence that shows that local populations depend upon remittances for local growth and that they circumnavigate the state and take little interest in direct state intervention (Eversole 2008). Fagen goes so far as to argue that the state is a drag on growth and development, arguing that in Haiti (among other places) the government has only contributed to growing problems and insecurity (Fagen 2006).

A third debate concerning the impacts of migration and remittance practices surrounds the issue of "brain drain," which is the assumption that migration robs a sending community or region of its workers, in particular, young, entrepreneurial workers (Tanner 2005). The decline in number of skilled workers and general manpower in a sending community leaves the community as little more than a nursery where future workers (who will join the migrant stream) are raised by the elderly, who will watch the children they have cared for leave.

Koser and van Hear (2003) note that the absence of migrants and the movement of refugees from their countries of origin leave a large gap that sometimes cannot be filled by remaining local workers and their skills. While remittances are an important outcome of migration, mobility robs a community of energy and skill and tends to emphasize the influence of the missing through their absence. The absence of a specific group in a community can become critical when a substantial portion of a population goes abroad, as has occurred in Afghanistan, Bosnia, El Salvador, and Eritrea. In 2001–2002, one in seven Afghans, one in ten Bosnians, and one in eleven Eritreans had left their homeland (Andrade-Eekhoff 2006; de Haas 2006b; Oruc 2009; Strand, Suhrke, and Harpviken 2004); and Andrade-Eekhoff notes that as many as 40 percent of El Salvador's citizens now live outside of the borders of their nation (2006). These are economically active people, with nearly all between the ages of 18 and 59 (Koser and van Hear 2003: 4–5). While the remittances of these movers are critical to the success of households and families left behind, it is nearly impossible to calculate the costs each family faces in response to migration. Not only are there emotional costs, but there are also social, cultural, and even economic costs as local patterns of labor and work are replaced. In rural Mexico, traditional labor practices become little more than a footnote from the past with little value and meaning as they are abandoned and replaced with the service jobs that migration promises (Cohen and Browning 2007).

The arguments around brain drain also focus on highly skilled migration and suggest that advanced countries attract those high-skilled and

trained professionals from less-developed and developing countries. Destination countries gain from the moves as educated professionals join the
nation as equals. However, countries of origin suffer as these movers tend
to leave and not look back even though transnational organizations and the
activities of their members make up for the loss over time.

The U.S. historically attracted highly skilled individuals from developed, developing, and less-developed parts of the world. High-tech industries in particular have pulled (or drained) IT professionals from Asia to fill
jobs that native-born citizens cannot fill. However, the issue is not a simple
one focused only on IT and the U.S. Higher education, for instance, pro-
motes similar kinds of moves as international faculty members and foreign
students have been cited as indicators of quality in many university rankings (Castells 1996:212).

As we have argued, brain drain is not necessarily about a lack of *any* job
opportunities, but rather involves a lack of *suitable* job opportunities for
the highly skilled that may lead to their emigration. For ambitious professionals with an eye on big salaries, staying in a low-income country may
create an environment of insecurity. Higher migration propensity is often
found among working-class and middle-class segments of middle-income
countries (Icduygu, Sirkeci, and Muradoglu 2001; Portes and Rumbaut
1996; Sassen 1998). Thus, it can be argued that these countries are likely to
benefit from transnationalization of specialty skills and the professionals
who practice them even as they lose populations to the pull of potential
jobs.

In a recent study of Indian entrepreneurs in Silicon Valley, Biradavolu
(2008) worked with men and women who ran software businesses with
global operations and significant Indian components in their ventures. For
many, globalization had forced them to move around the world. Explain-
ing his reasons for moving from India to the Silicon Valley of northern
California, Rajeev M. says, "I am here because this is where I can run the
best tech company in the world. . . . If I were into making toys, I would
go to China. If I wanted to grow coffee I would go to Brazil. . . . I am here
because this is where the money is, the resources. . . . I like living in California but that is not why I am here" (Biradavolu 2008:153). Subroto B.,
who spent many years in the U.S. and returned to Bangalore to co-found a
tech company there, says, "India is different from what it was before. The
reason I came back is because of opportunities here. Plus I am closer to my
extended family . . . but the other reason I am excited to be back here is
because I feel I can make a contribution" (Biradavolu 2008:155). He is talk-

ing about transferring the best of American business, including efficiency, a strong work ethic, and customer service, to India to create a better future.

These comments provide good examples of links between movers and nonmovers that can mitigate some of the pressures of brain drain. As the Indian entrepreneurs note above, entrepreneurs may expand their businesses into their country of origin or they may return and set up new businesses. The bottom line is the massive transfers that move through the transnational space: of funds—in the form of remittances or foreign direct investment—but, equally important, of knowledge—as facilitated by those highly skilled immigrants and returnees. Movers thus influence the lives of the nonmovers, not only because these professionals return to their home countries as entrepreneurs and invest there but also because they maintain and promote social and cultural ties with their host country and the country of origin (see Itzigsohn et al. 1999).

REMITTANCES, SECURITY, AND INSECURITY

A focus on security and insecurity in sending communities shifts us away from a focus on remittances in general and toward an approach that explores the role and value of remittances to specific social and cultural situations. Human security is a key concept for understanding human mobility because movers and nonmovers are security-seeking agents, among other things. Security and insecurity as well as the urge to seek security are based on individual-, household-, and community-level perceptions of the environment and decisions facing both movers and nonmovers. When people believe that their environments are becoming significantly insecure, then migration arises as a strategic option.

An environment of human insecurity does not simply occur in times of war and conflict; rather it can be characterized by lack of job opportunities, poor health and educational services, ethnic discrimination, political oppression, ethnic cleansing, or assimilationist policy and practices. Some of these factors are felt by individuals, others by a community or minority group. As such, certain groups of people may respond to security and insecurity through migration, and in these groups migration rates can increase dramatically.

Human insecurity is characterized by natural disasters, as we noted in the Haitian example. A second example is what occurred in southeast Asia on 26 December 2004, when an earthquake occurred in the Indian Ocean and the resulting tsunami caused more than 200,000 deaths and displaced over 1.7 million people (Gray et al. 2009). An environment of insecurity also arises from an individual's or household's circumstances. For example, in the traditional rural Kurdish communities of Eastern Turkey, blood feud (*kan davasi*) is a facilitator of migration. Families who are involved in blood feuds often leave their homes to avoid deaths due to long-running conflicts. Where the conflicts fester and build, violence is often the response, such as the mass killings that followed a wedding reception in Turkey; these killings were not random, nor associated with national politics, but instead were part of an ongoing feud between families (*The Guardian*, 5 May 2009). A similar tradition exists in Albania, and the collapse of the communist state appears to have led to an increase in blood feuds. These feuds are related to a three-thousand-year-old tradition (the *Kanun*) that developed in response to Albania's repeated conquests and lack of a centralized ruler (Mortimer and Toader 2005; Naegele 2001).

Individuals may feel restrained in particular locations or within their families and therefore opt to migrate as well. There are various reasons that an individual might choose to leave his family and swap the security of home for the insecurity that comes with migration. For example, a young artist in a rural location may feel that her options are so limited that there is no option but migration if she hopes to produce art. Gender relations also play a role in outcomes. The gay or transgendered individual may feel uncomfortable in a traditional small town. He or she may be the focus of ridicule and abuse, and there may be no way to live comfortably either in the open or closeted (Hammerton 2004). Young women often find that they are restricted in traditional, rural settings and cannot pursue education, careers, and independence at home (Plaza 2007). Migrating to an urban center or a well-known tolerant location in another country may be the only viable solution (McGhee 2003). Thus, the perception of the environment of human insecurity can be communal, but it is also personal, subjective, and relative.

In figure 6.1 we use a four-layer framework to illustrate the relationship of the various environments (from individual to the nation) in which security and insecurity may be contested. Security and insecurity are different at different levels and, as we have noted, can be classified as material and nonmaterial (Sirkeci 2006a). Among contributors to human insecurity are lack of job security (and lack of [suitable] employment opportunities), lack of food security, poor health services, paucity of educational opportunities, lack of personal security (e.g., presence of feud, war, clashes), restrictions

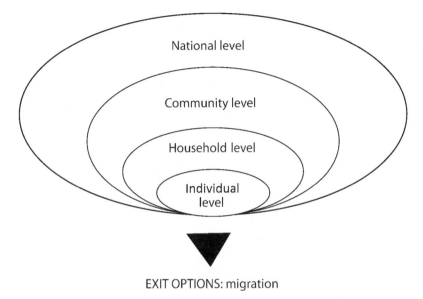

EXIT OPTIONS: migration

FIGURE 6.1.   *Environments of human insecurity.*

on ethnic, cultural, religious, and political rights and liberties for individuals as well as groups, environmental crises and disasters, and, finally, human conflicts (which range from small-scale disputes to violent feuds, and to warfare that can be internal and civil or international).

SECURITY AND REMITTANCES

Individuals, their families and households, and their communities seek security in different ways. Sometimes a search for security leads individuals to move from a rural hometown to an urban center within a country. Other times, they will cross borders, perhaps following the promise of security or at least a reduction in insecurity.

As a strategic option and a search for security, migration generates an inflow of goods and finances to the sending community. The contribution of these remittances to local or national development is a source of dispute in the social sciences. Some consider them as a key driver for development while others point out their contribution to consumerism but nothing else. Human security and insecurity, once adopted as a predictor of human mobility, can help us define the connection between movers and nonmovers through the flow of remittances.

International mobility is sometimes an outcome of an increased perception of risks (human insecurity) at home that can last for many years.[9] Over the years a culture of migration and the emergence of international migration can change a sending community and its environment. In other words, human insecurity at home can be reduced and sometimes alleviated with the help of remittances as well as a reduction in local populations who are competing for jobs. The benefits of this process are not just positive for the migrants and households involved, but for the wider origin community, as remitted funds are converted to local jobs and sometimes spent at local businesses.

Remittances can be economic, but as we have argued they are also at times nonmaterial in nature; noneconomic remittances can influence security and insecurity in sending communities. International migrants, refugees, and diasporic communities can be influential in changing the politics and policies of origin communities and countries. Iranian and Kurdish migrants in their diasporic communities exert such influences. Over the last three decades Turkish Kurds living abroad, mostly in Europe, have set up cultural and political associations, organized rallies and demonstrations, and continued promoting their language through publications and schools. One can see the impact of these efforts in the radical changes in the Turkish government's attitude towards its Kurdish minority. While the changes were not a result of pressures from the Kurdish community in Germany, they were influential. Furthermore, the influence of movers reaches beyond those who are members of ethnic minority populations. Turkish immigrants living in Western Europe have influenced Turkish politics and are a critical support for Turkey's case to join the European Union. The many Turkish-origin members of the European parliament as well as other national governments are critical to securing security for Turkish movers abroad as well as diminishing insecurity at home.

Remittances can alleviate poverty, enhance health status, and promote education in sending communities while boosting consumerism (Evans 1987; Hashim 2007; Hildebrandt and McKenzie 2006; WHO 2005).[10] Thus remittances are critical as nonmigrants work to reduce insecurity at home. While the role of remittances to control or mitigate insecurity is evident, remittances also foster mobility among future movers, and in the process may further reduce insecurity. There are cases where there is a fear (or an increase in insecurity) when new movers are anticipated. New movers may not remit, they may remit more than other movers, or they may simply exit the community and household. Nevertheless, generally remittances foster mobility and reduce insecurity (and see Conway and Cohen 1998). Thus, remittances are not just used to pay for school expenses and household improvements or to support local community services but also to facilitate further migration and future security (Massey et al. 1994).

FORMS OF CONTRIBUTION
OTHER THAN REMITTANCES

The migrants living in destination communities do more than send remittances and many of their activities may not be fully visible. They keep a sense or version of their native culture alive through language, schools, festivals, and celebrations. Political organizations and civic associations at points of destination also contribute to the communities their members have left behind and they can shape the future of their countries. Many countries that are home to large migrant populations allow those migrants who are away to participate in home country politics by voting in elections and party memberships. They contribute to charities. However, they also send home ideas, values, and cultural artifacts that Levitt (1998) describes as "social remittances." Social remittances play an important role in forming the transnational communities. They reproduce social ties and networks that link communities. The also have an impact on social and community development in sending communities as new ideas and possibilities are discovered, investments are made, and traditions are maintained. Levitt (2001) identifies three types of social remittances: normative structures, systems of practice, and social capital. The first refers to ideas, values, and beliefs that are influenced by migration and migrants as well as gender and generational relations. The second notes the ways in which agents engage with their world and its various locations; and the third notes the changing patterns of status.

The connections between sending and receiving countries are evident in the response of an interviewee to a Council of Europe project on migration and settlement:

> Being a diaspora resident in the Netherlands and in other
> Western countries, we are privileged to live in democratic
> societies and are thereby exposed to democratic political dealings and practices. This experience enables us to transfer or
> bring back valuable new political ideas and practices that can
> help the promotion of a democratic political life in Africa.
> (COE 2006:20)

This study of Ghanaians in the Netherlands and Cape Verdeans in Portugal reported that both African groups are actively involved in political reforms of political institutions and the democratization process in their respective home countries (ibid.: 21).

One should not assume that all remittance practices are positive. There are various positions for and against the impact of these contributions flowing back to the countries and communities of origin. While most remittances are positive for sending communities and countries, some others might be seen in a rather negative light. For a household, spending on luxury goods (defined locally) may seem a waste when there are critical daily expenses not met. Remittances can also impact national patterns when they fund rogue regimes and insurgent groups in home countries, particularly in less-developed countries. Again this is a contested area where the same flow can be considered positive or negative by different involved or interested parties. Such are the remittance flows between the Kurdish diaspora and respective guerilla groups in Turkey and neighboring countries. While pro-Kurdish parties may see this as a "peace-maker" or facilitator of democracy, for Turkish government and pro-Turkish parties this would be a clear "peace-wrecker."

CONCLUSIONS

Migration and development studies focus almost exclusively on less-developed and developing countries and the ways in which the immigrants who hail from such places can help their fellow nationals, who have been left behind on the ladder of development. Remittances are vital for these movers and the households and families they leave behind. Yet highly skilled migrants are also part of the equation, and their reasons for moving are likely different from those of their poorer neighbors; their remittance practices are also different.

And while most research is focused on the outcomes of migration and the impacts of remittance practices, we cannot forget the millions of dollars spent around the world legally and illegally to support movers, pay smugglers and human traffickers, and control and police border regions. From a business perspective, one might choose to regard every migrant as a cost to the government, a factor challenging national security and siphoning dollars that should go to native citizens and their needs. Yet we noted that destination countries earn millions of dollars from the efforts of migrants even as billions in remittances travel around the globe. Despite all the xenophobia in popular media and politics, immigrants contribute significantly to their host societies, and economically (if not publicly) they are welcome because the relatively lower wages they have to accept, along with limited securities (lack of unionization, being dependent on job-bound resident permits, etc.), appeal to many employers. Thus, understanding remittances needs to be more than searching for a single answer. Remittances solve problems for nonmovers even as migration creates problems for both origin and destination communities. We have argued that an approach that focuses on security and insecurity allows us to better capture the complicated and multifaceted nature of remittance practices.

CONCLUSIONS

What Alexis de Tocqueville saw in America was a society of immigrants, each of whom had begun life anew, on an equal footing. This was the secret of America: a nation of people with the fresh memory of old traditions who dared to explore new frontiers, people eager to build lives for themselves in a spacious society that did not restrict their freedom of choice and action.

    Immigration policy should be generous; it should be fair; it should be flexible. With such a policy we can turn to the world, and to our own past, with clean hands and a clear conscience.
— JOHN F. KENNEDY, *A NATION OF IMMIGRANTS*

John F. Kennedy's comments concerning migration capture the hope of a time in our collective history when most people believed immigrants were going to help the United States build a stronger future. There was great potential in their arrival, and we assumed that immigrants embraced their receiving nation, and the promises of the success that would come with their engagement in its growth and expansion. Nevertheless, for every hopeful statement on migration, we find an equally negative declaration, one that argues that immigrants are criminals, that they are focused on gaining wealth, or that they are trying to access education and attain rights to health care, retirement, and social supports. Often these are framed as abuses coming at an expense to the native-born. The critic continues by telling us that immigrants do not speak our language, do not worship the same god, and are not interested in participating in our national dialogue.

It is impossible to reconcile these positive and negative perspectives, and certainly neither fully captures the realities that face movers today. Actual experiences of migration are difficult to unwrap and understand. And it is probably much easier to simply demonize movers and blame them for all of the ills we face. Our goal should be to move away from caricatures of migrants (whether our stereotypes are positive or negative — compare Kennedy's statements with those of Theodore Roosevelt, which started Chapter 2) and explore the rise and meaning of migration, the place of internal and international movement, and the importance of remittances to everyday life, as we have attempted to do in this book.

To gain a better overall understanding of mobility we have combined a culture-of-migration approach with an appreciation of security and insecurity issues for contemporary movers. In this conclusion we briefly recapitulate our approach. In chapter 4 we noted that migration may have entered a new phase, and here we return to that point and consider just what the new phase of mobility may be.

A CULTURE OF MIGRATION

Our approach begins with the simple question that any potential mover must confront: Do I migrate? The question itself may not seem complicated, yet its answer will be complex and that response can send shock waves through households, families, and communities.

The question of mobility arises as a potential mover sees new opportunities outside of his or her immediate surroundings. It might be that the mover has encountered boundaries at home that limit her or his ability to successfully engage in work, social life, and local politics and chooses to head for an internal or international destination (Goodman and Hiskey 2008:206). Alternatively, a potential mover might recognize the opportunities that await the migrant regardless of his destination. Those destinations exert a strong pull, whether real or imagined, on the potential migrant and encourage movement with their promise of work, high wages, and new opportunities (Massey and Garcia 1987).

The decision to join the stream of migrants moving from rural to urban settings and crossing international borders is based on the strengths and abilities of the mover — her experiences, age, marital status, and education all influence outcomes and possibilities (Conway and Cohen 2002). Strengths and limits, capabilities and inabilities all combine to support the mover in her decision and to build an outcome that, it is hoped, will be positive for all involved.

Migration also has a profound impact on the migrant's household and family as well as the community he leaves behind. Nonmovers scramble to reorganize socially and to cope with the loss of an integral member of the socially constituted household. Child care and elder care may both be issues that face nonmovers. Nonmovers are challenged and must determine who will take care of animals, land, and communal demands for participation once the migrant has departed. In other words, nonmovers must cover for movers and juggle resources and requirements as they come; this is particularly difficult before a migrant's remittances begin to arrive.

The structure of migration, its history, and the continuity that characterizes movements past and present for most sending communities creates a "culture of migration" that supports movers and nonmovers and facilitates network building between origin and destination populations (Cohen 2004). New movers and potential migrants turn to friends and family for support. Migrants follow pathways to their destinations that were charted over years and with the input of earlier movers. Movers keep in touch with the families and households they left behind with the aid of ever-more complex cell phone networks, computer programs, and the constant movement of other people between origin and destination. Finally, the migrant supports his family through regular remittances. While we have noted that sometimes those remittances fail, and over time even the most regular of remittances decline, generally remittances play a critical role in the survival and maintenance of the sending household.

Security and insecurity issues are integral to understanding the process and development of migration and defining a culture-of-migration approach (Sirkeci 2009). Traditionally it was assumed that migrants fled insecurity at home to find security (or opportunity) abroad. Yet in the last chapter we argued that security and insecurity are dynamic and shift over space and time. While a lack of security can encourage migration, an overabundance of security can also restrict opportunities. New ways of thinking, contradictory gender roles, and new religious and political beliefs can be difficult to maintain in a traditional community. Thus, individuals may migrate to escape the security of home and gain new experiences, try new ways of living, and take chances.

Insecurity at home is an issue for many movers. We see the power of insecurity to motivate movement most clearly when we follow refugees, who are typically physically forced from their homes to camps and diasporic communities. In a sense, refugees struggle against at least three kinds of insecurity: at home; while in a camp; and when thrown into a new setting for resettlement. While there is no way to fully measure or quantify the level of insecurity that would motivate someone to join the ranks of refugees, we can clearly state that it is profound. The experience of losing security at home, fearing physical harm, and fleeing to a camp is nothing if not intense. Life needs to be difficult in the extreme to force people to abandon their homes, wealth, way of life, and links to place (Moorehead 2005).

A refugee trades everything he or she knows in response to a threat, some fear of harm, or sometimes a promise of a better future. The threat is usually one of extermination and death, while the promise may be of little more than a place to rest. Yet the refugee, with few choices and options, moves. Once away from the insecurity of home the refugee faces a new kind of insecurity. In a camp or center, waiting to return home or for an agreement to be struck in a conflict between antagonists, the refugee is in limbo. In the camp, insecurity is the threat to well-being and it comes with living without a history, without papers, and with few rights and privileges (Whittaker et al. 2006). Resettlement does not necessarily mean an end to insecurity, because it brings a new kind of insecurity when the culture, identity, and practices of the past come into conflict with the expectations of the destination country. And while many refugees are able to organize themselves and their communities in a way that reconstitutes their native systems, they are also challenged by the expectations, demands, and traditions of the destination country (Valentine, Sporton, and Nielsen 2009).

While the example of the refugee encapsulates the insecurity that comes with migration, most movers face similar challenges as they travel to internal or international destinations. Yet migrants decide to take the chance and face the challenges of moving. They transcend regional divisions, cultural traditions, and linguistic difference to find opportunities. In their destinations they often organize, creating transnational communities that link them to sending communities and anchor them in the traditional practices they have left behind (Vertovec 2009).

Regardless of the motivations for movement, remittances remain central to migration as a process. An overwhelming number of nonmigrants rely upon the work of friends and relatives to support them over time (Yang and Martínez 2006). Economic remittances help households survive and families maintain themselves even in the face of pressure that threatens their very survival (Cohen 2005). But as we have noted, remittances are more than economic, and they include goods and services, experiences, knowledge, and the like. These nonmonetary remittances are critical to a household's survival and maintenance over time. Nonmonetary remittances serve as social and cultural connections that become vital to sending households and the children of migrants.

A NEW PHASE FOR MIGRATION

The realities of contemporary migration are quite different from those encountered by migrants and movers from even a few decades in the past. The rural-to-urban shifts and industrial growth of the 1950s, 1960s, and 1970s that attracted many migrants to internal as well as international destinations has given way to migration that is driven by a growing demand for service workers in the West and declining economic opportunity in the Third World. The demand for labor, and specifically cheap labor, has driven migration and pulled unskilled workers to new destinations in Europe and the U.S. at the same time that neoliberal reforms have pushed rural peoples from their lands and toward urban centers and wage labor. Nowhere was the international dimension of this process more obvious than in the rise of Mexican migration to the U.S. (Delgado-Wise and Marquez Covarrubias 2007). In the same period, internal movers traveled from their hometowns in western China to work and start new lives in the coastal and industrial cities (Fan 2008).

The end of the twentieth century saw the continued growth of unskilled, service-based migration from south to north and east to west. The growth of migration brought national, ethnic, and minority populations into contact in new ways. Generally through the end of the twentieth century, native citizens saw the migrants living among them as necessary. Here were people willing to work for low wages and to do the jobs natives had left (Waldinger and Lichter 2003). At the same time, the migrant communities began to find their voices. They used their communities as a foundation to criticize their former nations (Fox and Rivera-Salgado 2004). They organized themselves to support their hometowns and they managed and coordinated their remittances to sustain their sending communities, build homes, and foster growth.

Yet the shift to service-based migration on a grand scale has not continued unabated in this new century. Nativist and anti-immigrant groups have always existed, and they have always objected to the presence and role of the migrant in native affairs (economic and otherwise). The events of 9/11 and the recessions of the last several years have only intensified the criticism of migrants and the calls for tighter borders, more restrictive laws, and more limitations on access to institutions ranging from schools to healthcare. The effects of heightened border security and the recession on migration are just now beginning to play themselves out, and migrants are caught in the center of the debate.

CONCLUSIONS

In this book we have put together a positive account of migration and offered positive models for understanding it. We place it within the framework of a dynamic conflict model, which is helpful for grasping the process (i.e., the fluid nature of migration). We also see mobility through the lens of households as collections of individuals with strong ties and joint decision-making processes. We emphasize a key element in migration processes, the nonmovers, who are often left outside the debate. By pointing out the links between movers and nonmovers we have tried to show that human mobility is not necessarily a problem for nonmovers (host and sending communities), because they are an integral part of the process.

The impacts of the renewed calls for tighter borders and the response of states to the global recession are two areas ripe for increased study. Through the 1990s and into the start of the twenty-first century migration was a relatively easy process for the mover. Migration was like a game of cat and mouse, with the migrant playing the role of the mouse who tries to avoid capture by the cat. Typically the mouse was able to avoid the cat, establish him- or herself, find a home and job, and work with little harassment.

At present, migrants are treated as criminals and capture often means deportation and a criminal record. We argue that it is time to worry less about legality and criminality and more about human rights. Legislating migration controls and in particular controls that limit access to public services will not lead to lower rates of migration, nor will they mitigate the impacts of the economic recession. Migrants are not a cause of these problems; rather they are a symptom of the inability of states to meet the needs of their populations. In a speech during his presidential campaign, then-senator Barack Obama said:

> Like millions of Americans, the immigrant story is also my story. My father came here from Kenya, and I represent a state where vibrant immigrant communities ranging from Mexican to Polish to Irish enrich our cities and neighborhoods. So I understand the allure of freedom and opportunity that fuels the dream of a life in the United States. But I also understand the need to fix a broken system.

Perhaps rather than projecting fear, we can embrace this diversity and challenge the status quo that defines migration as a problem.

NOTES

INTRODUCTION

Mojado, Spanish for "wet," is used negatively (in the chapter epigraph) to refer to Mexicans who must cross the Rio Grande (the river separating Mexico and the United States along the Texas-Mexico border). The term is pejorative and defines the Mexican migrant as undocumented—he or she cannot cross the border legally and instead is forced to sneak across the river, getting wet—*mojado*—as he or she enters the U.S. The premise that all Mexicans in the U.S. are *mojado*, or illegally in the country, leads to the assumption that because Mexicans are illegal, they are dangerous.

1. Fear of immigrants is often organized into anti-immigrant laws, such as SB1070 in the state of Arizona in 2010. SB1070 demands (among other things) that anyone who looks like an immigrant to a law enforcement officer must be able to show papers that prove his or her status as being legally in the U.S. (for details see the full bill at http://www.azleg.gov/legtext/49leg/2r/bills/sb1070s.pdf). Similarly, one can find dozens of examples from Europe where major political parties have increasingly promoted restrictive immigration policies, particularly in the last decade.

2. The United Nations reports that approximately 115 million migrants are currently living in developed countries (three quarters of the total are in 28 countries, with one in five in the U.S.) while about 75 million are in developing countries. The greatest increase in the number of international migrants over the last ten years has occurred in high-income destination countries, home to 41 million migrants (2006:13). Nevertheless, it is clear from the U.N.'s numbers that poorer countries host the vast majority of movers and in particular those forced out of their homelands as refugees.

3. It is difficult to estimate internal moves, particularly because these moves are often short term and can vary in distance. Even census data, which often detail the presence and absence of locally born individuals as well as those who have come to a place from outside, are not flawless. Typically, the numbers are a snapshot of

one particular time and note the mobility of local movers only at that given point, which is usually the date the census material was collected.

4. Government agencies are becoming more interested in tallying short-term migrations (i.e., less than one year but more than six months) within the overall count of international moves, as a recognition of increasing mobility, including long-distance, cross-border commutes (Sirkeci 2009).

5. Turks, Arabs, and Kurds (among others) are held to superficial national borders that were drawn at the end of World Wars I and II; these demarcations divided ethnic entities—an issue that we will return to in Chapter 4 and in our discussion of transnational space.

6. For details on the plight of the Uighurs, see Amnesty International's 2004 report "People's Republic of China: Uighurs fleeing persecution as China wages its 'war on terror,'" AI index: ASA 17/021/2004, available at www.amnesty.org (accessed 10 March 2009).

7. The strengths and weaknesses associated with the specific individual contribute to perceptions of security and insecurity for that person; these factors may be personal (what the individual can or cannot do), communal (for or against others who exhibit strengths and weaknesses), or global (placing migrants in situations where they may have to defend themselves against unknown threats). Perceptions of strengths and weaknesses, security and insecurity may be short-term and fleeting, or long-lasting. Strengths and weaknesses can challenge local beliefs and cultures of migration. They can also serve as foundations for future actions. The positive place the migrant holds in his or her sending community can strengthen his or her position in the social life of the new community. Yet at the same time, new ideas that migrants often bring with them as they return from destination communities can challenge traditional cultural practices.

8. Researchers have shown that migrants can and do fall for the myths (i.e., excessive wealth and success stories of earlier fellow migrants) they hear about destinations and benefits. But even in these situations, the potential migrant is making a calculated choice to move—although unfortunately her or his calculations are based on fallacies and a lack of background on the true outcomes of movements.

9. The idea of "nonmovers" is vexing in itself and suggests that migration is the norm for a population or people. Yet in nearly every situation migrants are outnumbered by those who never leave their hometown.

10. Contrary to most beliefs, over the course of several years of research with hundreds of families, Cohen encountered only one couple who had decided to migrate to try to access healthcare for their physically handicapped daughter. In fact, after staying in the U.S. for about six months, the family returned to their home in Oaxaca, having found it too difficult to gain coverage as undocumented migrants with a disabled child.

11. Similar examples can be drawn from relatively conservative and traditional societies, including Turkey and other Middle Eastern countries where women are subject to various limitations. In the process, many of these women found

themselves under extreme social pressures. Arranged marriages and honor killings among Muslim immigration populations in Western Europe are a few rather stark indicators of such pressures (Thapar-Björkert 2007).

12. We also include "luggage-traders" (also referred to as "trader-tourists" and "shuttle traders") from the Balkans and former Soviet Union countries, and other Eastern Europeans who visit Istanbul for very short terms to move goods back and forth (see Eder, Yakovlev, and Garkoglu 2003).

CHAPTER 1

The first chapter epigraph is from Schmalzbauer 2008:336. The second is cited in Sills 2007:4.

1. A real challenge to anthropological and geographic research is the fact that the human actors we study often do not perform as we might expect. It isn't that our models are wrong (and generally they are based on well-thought-out research and theory), but that humans are fundamentally unpredictable. While we need always to keep in mind that behaviors are hard to foresee, we should not abandon explanatory frameworks.

2. Taraneh Baniyaghoob reported that Iranian authorities approved a plan which forces all universities to admit local female students only if they have their fathers' or husbands' written permission. Although this appears to be an extreme case, it is important as we consider the strengths and weaknesses that limit decision making (see "Girls' Education in Main Cities' Universities Only with Their Parents' Written Permission," available at: http://ir-women.com/spip.php ?article7030).

3. A 2008 article appearing in the *Daily Mail* (online edition) described a survey in which nearly two-thirds of young people in Britain admitted to believing that immigrants "dilute" national identity, while a smaller percentage felt immigrants pose a security risk and challenge public order (http://www.dailymail .co.uk/news/article-1063195/Young-people-think-immigrants-threat-national-identity-jobs.html).

4. Early studies on gender and migration to the U.S. suggested that women are as likely as men to migrate to the U.S. However, they also emphasize that most migrant women are moving independently or as supporters of households—not as individuals (Curran et al. 2006:200–202).

5. Icudygu and Sirkeci note that "there were only 31 female workers registered among the total of 77,000 Turkish workers who arrived in Arab countries between 1967 and 1980" (1998:8).

6. Through the year 2000 nearly 80 percent of all U.S.-bound movers from the southern state of Oaxaca were men. Internal migration, or movement within Mexico's borders, was much more equitable, with just over one half of all migrants male (Cohen 2004). The phenomenon of very high levels of male migra-

tion in Oaxaca is quite unique compared to global international migration figures, which indicate an increasingly balanced distribution between men (50.4 percent) and women (49.6 percent) over the last four decades (Ratha and Shaw 2007).

7. Filipino international migration is also unique because of the high female domination in numbers. In 2001 it was reported that more than 90 percent of all overseas Filipino contract workers were women (Nadeau 2007:18).

8. Households also fail to function; there are many examples of households that cannot adapt to new situations and settings and there are certainly people who for one reason or another do not succeed within their households. Sometimes the failure may be criminal, but more often it is simply that the individual in question cannot or will not fill an intended role and the entire household suffers—as might the community. One older Oaxacan argued that migration was a great way to get rid of problematic individuals. If they stayed in their natal community they might sow dissent and unhappiness, but if they left as migrants, they would take their problems with them and away from the community (see Cohen 1999).

9. These costs may seem minimal from a Western perspective; however, from a local perspective, the costs of uniforms, supplies, and the like place a heavy burden on a family.

CHAPTER 2

1. A general model of assimilation assumes that over time an immigrant group will engage and join in with the dominant culture of its destination country (see Alba and Nee 1997 for discussion). This staged assimilation model contrasts with the segmented assimilation model that follows contemporary movers and notes that often migrants and in particular undocumented migrants do not necessarily assimilate into their larger destination societies (Waldinger and Lichter 2003). Instead, migrants often create ethnic enclaves in which they are isolated. Often they integrate in a downward fashion, joining the underclass (and see Zloniski 2006).

2. The website Moving Here follows the migration histories of Caribbean, Irish, Jewish, and South Asian people who settled in England (http://www.movinghere.org.uk/galleries/histories/default.htm).

3. The Chinese Exclusion Act of 1882 was perhaps the most significant anti-immigrant move by the U.S. government, restricting entry to the U.S. for Chinese immigrants looking for work in gold mines, among other areas (and see Gyory 1998).

4. A perspective that defines people as generally followers rather than agents involved in the creation of social life and cultural patterns of beliefs dominates much of the literature in migration (and the social sciences in general) through the mid-twentieth century. For our purposes, this makes it difficult to define and describe transnational processes; nevertheless, we should assume they were present.

5. Foreign-born make up about 10 percent of the contemporary U.S. population.

6. In places like Venezuela, Europeans would arrive as immigrants and "whiten" the country. Governments assumed that the very presence of European immigrants would develop and modernize the backward-looking peasants who dominated the state.

7. "Refugee" is a catchall category that includes those fleeing war and ethnic clashes as well as those fleeing natural disasters. Internal refugees lack international recognition even though they face terrible situations, and disaster refugees are fleeing natural or manmade events that threaten their life and traditions. They are widely called internally displaced people (IDPs).

8. An Iranian American journalist, Yaghmaian (2005) wrote vivid memories of his trips with Muslim migrants from Iran who were trying to go through Turkish, Bulgarian, Greek, and Albanian borders, where many lives were lost.

9. See the Minute Men website at http://www.minutemanhq.com/.

CHAPTER 3

The chapter epigraph is from Fan and Wenfei 2008:220.

1. This was the area known historically as Inner Mongolia and is contrasted with Outer Mongolia, a region independent of Chinese control.

2. Migration intensity is computed by expressing the total number of migrants as a percentage of the population at risk in a certain period of time.

3. Salzburg was also a key destination for Germans from the German Reich (Jordan 2006:65–73).

4. The U.S. Census noted that the average commute in the U.S. overall was just over 24 minutes in 2004 and nearly 42 minutes in Queens, New York. While maybe not an obvious migration, these commutes do emphasize the daily mobility that characterizes citizens in some of the larger metro areas of the U.S. (see http://www.census.gov/newsroom/releases/archives/american_community_survey_acs/cb05-ac02.html).

5. There is evidence that not only in Britain but also in the Ottoman Empire there were significant rural-to-urban internal migrations dating back to the thirteenth and fourteenth centuries in the former and the fifteenth and sixteenth centuries in the latter. In fact, in 1567 the Ottoman sultan issued a law to prohibit migration from the provinces to Istanbul (Gümüşçü 2004:242).

6. See, for example, Kristy Walker's *Daily Mail* (online edition) article "Lancashire Tops Britain's Yob Culture 'League Table of Shame'" at http://www.daily mail.co.uk/news/article-1199542/Lancashire-tops-Britains-yob-culture-league-table-shame.html (14 July 2009).

CHAPTER 4

The first chapter epigraph is from *From the Old Country* (Stave, Sutherland, and Salerno 1994:58). The second chapter epigraph is found in *Ellis Island Interviews* (Coan 1997).

1. Fix et al. (2009) note that, regardless of the rhetoric concerning undocumented migration, only about 10–11 percent of international movers travel without papers and documentation.

2. Eric Wolf (1982) moves the discussion beyond Mintz's interest in sugar and shows how population mobility and immobility engage with colonial expansion worldwide. A challenge for us as we try to understand migration outcomes and the impacts of forced and free mobility on native populations is that most histories are written about the drivers of expansion, not the actors who are involved locally.

3. Migrants who travel alone, making decisions independently of others, are nevertheless making decisions that have an impact on the well-being of their households.

4. Any model of migration that reduces the motivation for border crossing to one variable—whether this be economic, political, or cultural—is simplifying a very difficult and complicated decision and process.

5. In fact, there is little overall impact even for natives who would likely hold the jobs that immigrants fill upon their arrival (Friedberg and Hunt 1995).

6. It is interesting that debates about migrants driving down wages do not often refer to highly skilled migrants. Rather, the alarm is almost always sounded about the problems that face unskilled workers. Of course, the majority of immigrants fill unskilled positions, yet the lack of interest in highly skilled immigration as an issue may be one indication that the criticisms are motivated by political interests rather than any real interest in migration reform.

7. Filipino nurses are recruited informally to the U.S., yet several bills have been introduced (including the Nursing Relief Act of 2009—H.R. 1001) to bring as many as 50,000 nurses to the U.S. with special visas.

8. Neoliberal reforms shift economic control from the public to private sector with the goal of increased efficiency and improved economic indicators at a national level. While neoliberal reforms often do lead to improved national economic performance, regional differences can be extreme and rural poverty often increases (see Gledhill 1995).

9. http://www.radiobilingue.org/archive.

10. Ocalan is still in prison, and the death penalty was abolished in Turkey in the early 2000s.

CHAPTER 5

The epigraph is quoted in Trisal 2007:104.

1. Even when using terms like "nonmigrant" and "stay-at-home" we are still able to talk about mobility. For instance, nonmigrants commute and follow daily circuits between a home and place of work.

2. Immigrants and citizens alike may face discrimination because they "look like" a member of a marked ethnic/minority group. In several countries citizenship remains problematic for children of immigrants, who even after a number of generations may not have full rights.

CHAPTER 6

The second chapter epigraph is taken from a quote in Eames Roebling and Silveira 2009.

1. Conway (2007) notes that these demands usually increase as migrants return and bring with them new ideas for living that influence home design, learned values, and job seeking, among other things.

2. International movers, particularly those from ethnic and linguistic minority groups, are often abused by smugglers (*coyotes*) and find they have become modern-day slaves to the *coyotes* and employers they had chosen to trust. Southern California farmers are infamous for abusing non-Spanish-speaking native workers they recruit from the south of Mexico. These indigenous migrants find themselves caught in a virtual migratory limbo. They are undocumented, non-Spanish-, non-English-speakers who fear capture by U.S. border forces; they often sign exploitative contracts that leave them indentured to their employees; and they are often kept isolated and far from co-nationals and others who might help them (see Nangengast, Stavenhagen, and Kearney 1992). The militarization of borders also ensnares middle-class movers, who may pay thousands of dollars to cross frontiers. Andrade-Eekhoff notes that middle-class El Salvadorians often pay $3,000 or more to cross into the U.S. with the hopes of finding social and economic security in their new home (2006).

3. A migrant may earn the equivalent of a day's wage in a sending country in an hour or sometimes less in the destination country. The margin can be much smaller in financial terms for some relatively wealthier origin countries, but in terms of human security and insecurity, the perceived differences and opportunities are considered an important bonus (and see Heyman 2007).

4. Deductions are made for taxes and other expenses, including healthcare and, in the U.S., Social Security. In fact, Duleep and Dowhan estimated that in one year $6 billion flowed from the wages of undocumented migrant workers to the U.S. Social Security Administration (2008).

5. Moses and Letnes' argument (2003) focuses on free migration, which they

argue generates an efficiency gain (or a gain in earnings in relation to costs) as high as $3.4 trillion.

6. Cliggett (2005) also notes that the absence of movers from a household reduces the burden on their sending household and thus enhances a household's ability to support those nonmovers left behind.

7. The January 2010 earthquake again devastated Haiti. In response the World Bank estimates that remittances may increase by as much as 20 percent, or approximately $360 million (see http://wwww.reliefweb.int/rw/rwb.nsf/db900 SID/EGUA-85JQKL?OpenDocument).

8. The *Tres-por-Uno* program is a success in Mexico, yet remains underfunded. Furthermore, as Staffon (2006) notes, funding is unevenly spread across the country, going to traditional sending regions and avoiding new sending states as well as those states that are home to political unrest, like Chiapas.

9. While conflicts can erupt suddenly and natural disasters are often unanticipated, social disputes, poverty, and marginality are often rooted in long-term, systemic problems.

10. While we emphasize positive outcomes in our discussion, migration can also create health crises and open the door for infection and disease. Evans notes that migration can bring AIDS, among other health crises, to communities ill prepared to cope with such a scourge (1987).

REFERENCES

ABU-EI-HAJ, THEA RENDA

2007   Educating for democratic citizenship in an era of transnational migration and global conflict. *Harvard Educational Review* 77.3:285–316.

ACOSTA, P., ET AL.

2006   Remittances and development in Latin America. *World Economy* 29.7:957–987.

ADAMS, RICHARD H., JR.

1989   Worker remittances and inequality in rural Egypt. *Economic Development and Cultural Change* 38.1:45–71.

1996   Remittances, inequality, and asset accumulation: The case of rural Pakistan. In *Development strategy, employment, and migration: Country experiences*, ed. D. O'Connor and L. Farsakh, 149–170. Paris: OECD.

2006   International remittances and the household: Analysis and review of global evidence. *Journal of African Economies* 15 (supplement): 396–425.

ADAMS, RICHARD H., JR., AND JOHN PAGE

2005   Do international migration and remittances reduce poverty in developing countries? *World Development* 33.10:1645–1669.

ADELMAN, ROBERT M., AND STEWART E. TOLNAY

2003   Occupational status of immigrants and African Americans at the beginning and end of the Great Migration. *Sociological Perspectives* 46:179–206.

ALBA, RICHARD, AND VICTOR NEE

1997   Rethinking assimilation theory for a new era of immigration. *International Migration Review* 31.4:826–875.

ALI, SYED

2007   "Go West, young man": The culture of migration among Muslims in Hyderabad, India. *Journal of Ethnic and Migration Studies* 33.1:37–58.

AL-SHARMANI, MULKI

2006   Living transnationally: Somali diasporic women in Cairo. *International Migration* 44.1:55–77.

AMERY, HUSSEIN ABDUL-MUNIM

1992   *The effects of migration and remittances on two Lebanese villages.* Ph.D. diss., McMaster University, Canada.

ANBINDER, TYLER

1992   *Nativism and slavery: The Northern know-nothings and the politics of the 1850s.* New York: Oxford University Press.

ANDRADE-EEKHOFF, KATHARINE

2006   Migration and development in El Salvador: Ideals versus reality. Washington, DC: Migration Information Source. http://www.migration information.org/Feature/display.cfm?ID=387.

BADE, KLAUS J.

2003   *Migration in European history.* Trans A. Brown. Malden, MA: Blackwell.

BASCH, LINDA G., N. GLICK SCHILLER, AND C. S. BLANC, EDS.

1994   *Nations unbound: Transnational projects, postcolonial predicaments, and deterritorialized nation-states.* Amsterdam: Gordon and Breach Science.

BEAN, FRANK D., ET AL.

1998   The quantification of migration between Mexico and the United States. In *Migration between Mexico and the United States*, vol. I, 1–90. Austin: Mexican Ministry of Foreign Affairs and the United States Commission on Immigration Reform.

BELL, MARTIN, AND SALUT MUHIDIN

2009   Cross-national comparison of internal migration. Human Development Reports, Research Paper 2009/30. United Nations Development Program.

BINFORD, LEIGH

2003   Migrant remittances and (under)development in Mexico. *Critique of Anthropology* 23.3:305–336.

BIRADAVOLU, MONICA RAO

2008   *Indian entrepreneurs in Silicon Valley: The making of a transnational technocapitalist class.* Amherst, NY: Cambria Press.

BLANK, REBECCA M., SHELDON DANZIGER, AND ROBERT F. SCHOENI

2006   *Working and poor: How economic and policy changes are affecting low-wage workers.* New York: Russell Sage Foundation.

BOEHM, DEBORAH A.

2008   "For my children": Constructing family and navigating the state in the U.S.–Mexico transnation. *Anthropological Quarterly* 81.4:777–802.

BORJAS, GEORGE J.

1999   *Heaven's door.* Princeton: Princeton University Press.

2003   The economic integration of immigrants in the United States: Lessons for policy. UNU-WIDER Discussion Papers 2003/78. Helsinki: World Institute for Development Economics Research.

2006   Native internal migration and the labor market impact of immigration. *Journal of Human Resources* 41.2:221–258.

BOSHYK, YURY, WSEVOLOD W. ISAJIW, AND ROMAN SENKUS

1992   *The refugee experience: Ukrainian displaced persons after World War II.* Edmonton: Canadian Institute of Ukrainian Studies, University of Alberta.

BOUGUE, DONALD J.

1977   A migrant's eye view of the costs and benefits of migration to a metropolis. In *Internal Migration: A comparative perspective*, ed. A. A. Brown and E. Neuberger, 167–182. New York: Academic Press.

BOURDIEU, PIERRE

1977   *Outline of a theory of practice.* Trans. R. Nice. Cambridge: Cambridge University Press.

BOVENKERK, FRANK

1982   Why returnees generally do not turn out to be "agents of change": The case of Suriname. In *Return migration and remittances: Developing a Caribbean perspective*, ed. W. F. Stinner, K. De Albuquerque, and R. S. Bryce-Laporte, 183–216. RIIES Occasional Papers 3. Washington, DC: Research Institute on Immigration and Ethnic Studies, Smithsonian Institution.

BRETTELL, CAROLINE B.

1995   *We have already cried many tears: The stories of three Portuguese migrant women.* Prospect Heights, IL: Waveland Press.

BROWER, DANIEL

1996   Russian roads to Mecca: Religious tolerance and Muslim pilgrimage in the Russian empire. *Slavic Review* 55.3:567–584.

BROWN, RICHARD P. C., AND J. CONNELL

1994   The global flea market: Migration, remittances, and the informal economy in Tonga. *Development and Change* 24.4:611–647.

BRUMER, ANITA

2008   Gender relations in family-farm agriculture and rural–urban migration in Brazil. *Latin American Perspectives* 35.6:11–28.

BUCKLEY, MARY, ED.

1997   *Post-Soviet women: From the Baltic to Central Asia.* Cambridge: Cambridge University Press.

BUCKLEY, RALF

2005   Social trends and ecotourism: Adventure recreation and amenity migration. *Journal of Ecotourism* 4.1:56–61.

CAPPUCCIO, FRANCESCO P., AND STEVEN W. LOCKLEY

2008   Safety and the flying doctor. *British Medical Journal* 336:218.

CARLING, JORGEN
2008   The determinants of migrant remittances. *Oxford Review of Economic Policy* 24.3:581–598.

CARR, DAVID
2009   Population and deforestation: Why rural migration matters. *Progress in Human Geography* 33.3:355–378.

CARTON DE GRAMMONT, HUBERT, AND SARA MARIA LARA FLORES
2010   Productive restructuring and "standardization" in Mexican horticulture: Consequences for labour. *Journal of Agrarian Change* 10.2:228–250.

CASTELLS, MANUEL
1996   *Rise of the network society.* Cambridge, MA: Blackwell.

CASTLES, STEPHEN
2009   Development and migration—migration and development: What comes first? Global perspective and African experiences. *Theoria: A Journal of Social and Political Theory* 56 (121): 1–31.

CAVALLI-SFORZA, LUIGI L., AND FRANCESCO CAVALLI-SFORZA
1995   *The great human diasporas: A history of diversity and evolution.* Reading, MA: Addison-Wesley.

CERRUTTI, MARCELA, AND DOUGLAS S. MASSEY
2001   On the auspices of female migration from Mexico to the United States. *Demography* 38.2:187–200.

CHAPMAN, ADAM
2004   Music and digital media across the Lao diaspora. *Asia Pacific Journal of Anthropology* 5.2:129–144.

CHAVEZ, LEO R.
1994   The power of the imagined community: The settlement of undocumented Mexicans and Central Americans in the United States. *American Anthropologist* 96.1:52–73.

CHOMSKY, AVIVA
2007   *"They take our jobs!": And twenty other myths about immigration.* Boston: Beacon Press.

CHRISTOPHER, EMMA, CASSANDRA PYBUS, AND MARCUS B. REDIKER
2007   *Many middle passages: Forced migration and the making of the modern world.* Berkeley: University of California Press.

CLARK, WILLIAM KAMALOV, AND ABLET KAMALOV
2004   Uighur migration across central Asian frontiers. *Central Asian Survey* 23.2:167–182.

CLIGGETT, LISA
2000   Social components of migration: Experiences from Southern Province, Zambia. *Human Organization* 59.1:125–135.

2003 Gift remitting and alliance building in Zambian modernity: Old answers to modern problems. *American Anthropologist* 105.3:543–552.

2005 Remitting the gift: Zambian mobility and anthropological insights for migration studies. *Population, Space, and Place* 11.1:35–48.

COAN, PETER M.

1997 *Ellis Island interviews: In their own words.* New York: Facts on File.

COCKERTON, CAMILLA

1996 Less a barrier, more a line: The migration of Bechuanaland women to South Africa, 1850–1930. *Journal of Historical Geography* 22.3:291–307.

COE (COUNCIL OF EUROPE)

2006 Migration and co-development, case studies: Netherlands and Portugal, social remittances of the African diasporas in Europe. Lisbon: North-South Centre of the Council of Europe.

COHEN, DEBORAH

2006 From peasant to worker: Migration, masculinity, and the making of Mexican workers in the U.S. *International Labor and Working-Class History* 69.1:81–103.

COHEN, JEFFREY H.

1999 *Cooperation and community: Economy and society in Oaxaca.* Austin: University of Texas Press.

2002 Migration and "stay-at-homes" in rural Oaxaca, Mexico: Local expression of global outcomes. *Urban Anthropology* 31.1:231–259.

2004 *The culture of migration in southern Mexico.* Austin: University of Texas Press.

2005 Remittance outcomes and migration: Theoretical contests, real opportunities. *Studies in International Comparative Development* 40.1:88–112.

2007 The role of crises in migration outcomes: Rural Oaxacans and politics in Oaxaca City, Mexico. *Population Review* 46.2:22–31.

COHEN, JEFFREY H., ET AL.

2003 A local approach to the study of transnational processes: Survey ethnography in the central valley of Oaxaca, Mexico. *Field Methods* 15.4:366–385.

COHEN, JEFFREY H., AND ANJALI BROWNING

2007 The decline of a craft: Basket making in San Juan Guelavia, Oaxaca. *Human Organization* 66.3:229–239.

COHEN, JEFFREY H., RICHARD JONES, AND DENNIS CONWAY

2005 Why remittances shouldn't be blamed for rural underdevelopment in Mexico. *Critique of Anthropology* 25.1:87–96.

COHEN, JEFFREY H., LEILA RODRIGUEZ, AND MARGARET FOX

2008 Gender and migration in the central valleys of Oaxaca, Mexico. *International Migration* 46.1:79–101.

COHEN, JEFFREY H., AND IBRAHIM SIRKECI

2005   A comparative study of Turkish and Mexican transnational migration outcomes: Facilitating or restricting immigrant integration? In *Crossing over: Comparing recent migration in the United States and Europe*, ed. H. Henke, 147–162. Lanham: Rowman & Littlefield.

CONWAY, DENNIS

2000   Notions unbound: A critical (re)reading of transnationalism suggests that U.S.-Caribbean circuits tell the story better. In *Theoretical and methodological issues in migration research: Interdisciplinary, intergenerational, and international perspectives*, ed. B. Agozino, 203–226. Aldershot: Ashgate.

2007   The importance of remittances for the Caribbean's future transcends their macroeconomic influences. *Global Development Studies* 4.3–4:41–76.

CONWAY, DENNIS, AND JEFFREY H. COHEN

1998   Consequences of return migration and remittances for Mexican transnational communities. *Economic Geography* 74.1:26–44.

2002   Local dynamics in multi-local, transnational spaces of rural Mexico: Oaxacan experiences. *International Journal of Population Geography* 9.1:141–161.

CONWAY, DENNIS, AND ROBERT B. POTTER

2007   Caribbean transnational return migrants as agents of change. *Geography Compass* 1.1:25–45.

CORDELL, DENNIS D.

1996   *Hoe and wage: A social history of a circular migration system in West Africa*. Boulder: Westview.

CORNELIUS, WAYNE A., ET AL.

2008   Controlling unauthorized immigration from Mexico: The failure of "prevention through deterrence" and the need for comprehensive reform. Immigration Policy Center. http://www.immigrationforum.org/images/uploads/CCISbriefing061008.pdf.

CORNELIUS, WAYNE A., THOMAS J. ESPENSHADE, AND IDEAN SALEHYAN, EDS.

2001   *The international migration of the highly skilled: Demand, supply, and development consequences in sending and receiving countries*. La Jolla: Center for Comparative Immigration Studies, University of California, San Diego.

COUTIN, SUSAN BIBLER

2007   *Nations of emigrants: Shifting boundaries of citizenship in El Salvador and the United States*. Ithaca: Cornell University Press.

CRÉPEAU, FRANÇOIS, ET AL., EDS.

2006   *Forced migration and global processes: A view from forced migration studies*. Lanham: Lexington Books.

CUBAN, SONDRA
2009   Skilled immigrant women careers in rural England and their downward mobility. *Migration Letters* 6.2:177–184.

CURRAN, SARA R., ET AL.
2006   Mapping gender and migration in sociological scholarship: Is it segregation or integration? *International Migration Review* 40.1:199–223.

DAHRENDORF, RALF
1959   *Class and class conflict in industrial society.* Stanford: Stanford University Press.

DE HAAS, HEIN
2006a   Migration, remittances, and regional development in southern Morocco. *Geoforum* 37.4:565–571.
2006b   Trans-Saharan migration to North Africa and the EU: Historical roots and current trends. Washington, DC: Migration Information Source. http://www.migrationinformation.org/feature/display.cfm?id=484.

DELGADO-WISE, RAUL, AND HUMBERTO MARQUEZ COVARRUBIAS
2007   The reshaping of Mexican labor exports under NAFTA: Paradoxes and challenges. *International Migration Review* 41.3:656–679.

DEMIR, IPEK, AND WELAT ZEYDANLIOGLU
2010   On the representation of "others" at Europe's borders: The case of Iraqi Kurds. *Journal of Contemporary European Studies* 18.1:7–23.

DINÇER, BÜLENT, METIN ÖZASLAN, AND ERDOĞAN SATILMIŞ
1996   İllerin sosyo-ekonomik gelişmişlik sıralaması araştırması [A survey of socioeconomic rankings by province]. Ankara: DPT. Bölgesel Gelişme ve Yapısal Uyum Genel Müdürlüğü.

DONATO, KATHERINE M., ET AL.
2006   A glass half full? Gender in migration studies. *International Migration Review* 40.1:3–26.

DONATO, KATHARINE M., BRANDON WAGNER, AND EVELYN PATTERSON
2008   The cat and mouse game at the Mexico-U.S. border: Gendered patterns and recent shifts. *International Migration Review* 42.2:330–359.

DOUGLASS, MIKE, AND GLENDA S. ROBERTS, EDS.
2000   *Japan and global migration: Foreign workers and the advent of a multicultural society.* London: Routledge.

DOUGLASS, WILLIAM A.
1970   Peasant emigrants: Reactors or actors? In *Migration and anthropology. Proceedings of the 1970 annual spring meeting of the American Ethnological Society,* ed. R. F. Spencer, 21–35. Seattle: American Ethnological Society and the University of Washington Press.

DREBY, JOANNE
    2006   Honor and virtue—Mexican parenting in the transnational context. *Gender and Society* 20.1:32–59.

DULEEP, HARRIET ORCUTT, AND DANIEL J. DOWHAN
    2008   Research on immigrant earnings. *Social Security Bulletin* 68.1. http://www
    .ssa.gov/policy/docs/ssb/v68n1/68n1p31.html.

DURAND, JORGE
    2007   *Braceros: Las miradas mexicana y estadounidense. Antología (1945–1964).* Mexico:
    Miguel Ángel Porrúa.

DUSTMANN, CHRISTIAN, AND IAN PRESTON
    2001   Attitudes to ethnic minorities, ethnic context, and location decisions.
    Economic Journal 111 (470): 353–373.

EAMES ROEBLING, ELIZABETH, AND TOVE SILVEIRA
    2009   Dominican Republic: Remittance crunch, but women migrants keep
    sending. Inter Press Service News Agency. http://ipsnews.net/news.asp
    ?idnews=47424.

EDER, M., A. YAKOVLEV, AND A. GARKOGLU
    2003   Suitcase trade between Turkey and Russia: Microeconomics and institu-
    tional structure. Preprint WP4/2003/07. Moscow: SU-HSE.

EVANS, JEFFREY
    1987   Migration and health. *International Migration Review* 21.3: v–xiv.

EVERSOLE, ROBYN
    2008   Development in motion: What to think about migration? *Development in
    Practice* 18.1:94–99.

FAGEN, PATRICIA
    2006   Remittances in crises: A Haiti case study. HPG Background Paper. Lon-
    don: Humanitarian Policy Group. http://www.odi.org.uk/resources/
    download/300.pdf.

FAIST, THOMAS
    1997   The crucial meso-level. In *International migration, immobility, and devel-
    opment: Multidisciplinary perspectives,* ed. T. Hammar, G. Brochmann,
    K. Tamas, and T. Faist, 187–218. New York: Berg.
    2000a *The volume and dynamics of international migration in transnational social space.*
    Oxford: Oxford University Press.
    2000b Transnationalization in international migration: Implications for the
    study of citizenship and culture. *Ethnic and Racial Studies* 23.2:189–222.

FAN, C. CINDY
    2008a *China on the move: Migration, the state, and the household.* London:
    Routledge.
    2008b Migration, hukou, and the Chinese city. In *China urbanizes: Conse-*

quences, strategies, and policies, ed. S. Yusuf and A. Saich, 65–90. Washington, DC: World Bank.

FAN, C. CINDY, AND WINNIE WANG WENFEI

2008   The household as security: Strategies of rural–urban migrants in China. In *Migration and social protection in China*, ed. R. Smyth and I. Nielsen, 205–243. New York: World Scientific.

FAWCETT, JOHN, AND VICTOR TANNER

2002   The internally displaced people of Iraq. SAIS Project on Internal Displacement, Occasional Paper. Washington, D.C: Brookings Institution. http://www.brookings.edu/~/media/Files/rc/papers/2002/10iraq_fawcett/iraqreport.pdf.

FERGUSON, PHYLLIS

2010   IDP camp closure and gender inequality in Timor-Leste. *Forced Migration Review* 34:67–69.

FERNÁNDEZ DE CASTRO, RAFAEL, ET AL., EDS.

2006   *El programa 3 × 1 para migrantes: ¿Primera política transnacional en México?* Mexico: Instituto Tecnológico Autónomo de México/Universidad Autónoma de Zacatecas/Miguel Ángel Porrúa.

FISCHER, PETER A., REINER MARTIN, AND THOMAS STAUBHAAR

1997   Should I stay or should I go? In *International migration, immobility, and development: Multidisciplinary perspectives*, ed. T. Hammar, G. Brochmann, K. Tamas, and T. Faist, 49–90. New York: Berg.

FIX, MICHAEL, ET AL.

2009   *Migration and the global recession*. Washington, DC: Migration Policy Institute.

FMO (FORCED MIGRATION ONLINE)

n.d.   What is forced migration? http://www.forcedmigration.org/whatisfm.htm.

FOMBY, PAULA

2005   *Mexican migrants and their parental households in Mexico*. New York: LFB Scholarly Publishing.

FORTES, MEYER

1971   Introduction. In *The development cycle in domestic groups*, ed. J. Goody, 1–15. Cambridge: Cambridge University Press.

FOX, JONATHAN

2007   Rural democratization and decentralization at the state/society interface: What counts as "local" government in the Mexican countryside? *Journal of Peasant Studies* 34.3:527–559.

FOX, JONATHAN, AND GASPAR RIVERA-SALGADO, EDS.

2004   *Indigenous Mexican Migrants in the United States*. San Diego: University of

California Press, the Center for U.S.-Mexican Studies, and the Center for Comparative Immigration Studies.

FREEDMAN, JANE

2004   *Immigration and insecurity in France.* Aldershot: Ashgate.

FRIEDBERG, RACHEL M., AND JENNIFER HUNT

1995   The impact of immigrants on host country wages, employment, and growth. *Journal of Economic Perspectives* 9.2:23–44.

FUGLERUD, OIVIND, AND ADA ENGEBRIGTSEN

2006   Culture, networks, and social capital: Tamil and Somali immigrants in Norway. *Ethnic and Racial Studies* 29.6:1118–1134.

GAMBURD, MICHELE R.

2008   Milk teeth and jet planes: Kin relations in families of Sri Lanka's transnational domestic servants. *City and Society* 20.1:5–31.

GAMIO, MANUEL

1969   *El inmigrante mexicano: La historia de su vida.* Mexico: Universidad Nacional Autonoma de Mexico.

GAMMAGE, SARAH

2006   Exporting people and recruiting remittances: A development strategy for El Salvador? *Latin American Perspectives* 33.6:75–100.

GARLAND, SARAH

2009   *Gangs in Garden City: How immigration, segregation, and youth violence are changing America's suburbs.* New York: Nation Books.

GEDIK, AYSE

2003   Differential urbanization in Turkey: 1955–2000. 43rd Congress of the European Regional Science Association, Jyväskylä, Finland.

GEORGES, EUGENIA

1992   Gender, class, and migration in the Dominican Republic: Women's experiences in a transnational community. In *Towards a transnational perspective on migration: Race, class, ethnicity, and nationalism reconsidered,* ed. N. Glick Schiller, L. Basch, and C. Blanc-Szanton, 81–99. New York: Annals of the New York Academy of Sciences.

GERSTLE, GARY

1999   Liberty, coercion, and the making of Americans. In *The handbook of international migration: The American experience,* ed. C. Hirschman, P. Kasinitz, and J. DeWind, 275–293. New York: Russell Sage Foundation.

GIBNEY, MATTHEW J., AND RANDALL HANSEN, EDS.

2005   *Immigration and Asylum: From 1900 to the Present.* Santa Barbara, CA: ABC-CLIO.

GILBERTSON, GRETA A.

1995   Women's labor and enclave employment: The case of Dominican and

Colombian women in New York City. *International Migration Review* 29.3:657–670.

GLAZIER, IRA A., AND MICHAEL TEPPER

1983   *The Famine immigrants: Lists of Irish immigrants arriving at the port of New York, 1846-1851.* Baltimore: Genealogical Publisher Company.

GLEDHILL, JOHN

1995   *Neoliberalism, transnationalization, and rural poverty: A case study of Michoacán, Mexico.* Boulder: Westview.

GLICK SCHILLER, N., L. BASCH, AND C. BLANC-SZANTON, EDS.

1992   *Towards a transnational perspective on migration: Race, class, ethnicity, and nationalism reconsidered.* New York: New York Academy of Sciences.

GONZALEZ, DENISE

2009   Beyond remittances: Hometown associations as a mechanism for immigrant political incorporation in the United States. Paper presented at the annual meeting of the Midwest Political Science Association, Chicago, 25 May 2009. http://www.allacademic.com/meta/p_mla_apa_research _citation/1/3/7/1/0/p137104_index.html.

GONZÁLEZ, NANCIE L. SOLIEN

1988   *Sojourners of the Caribbean: Ethnogenesis and ethnohistory of the Garifuna.* Urbana: University of Illinois Press.

GOODMAN, GARY L., AND JONATHAN T. HISKEY

2008   Exit without leaving—Political disengagement in high-migration municipalities in Mexico. *Comparative Politics* 40.2:169–188.

GOODY, JACK

1972   The evolution of the family. In *Household and family in past times*, ed. P. Laslett and R. Wall, 103–124. Cambridge: Cambridge University Press.

GRAY, CLARK, ET AL.

2009   Population displacement and mobility in Sumatra after the tsunami. Paper presented at IUSSP Congress, Marrakech, Morocco.

GREGORY, JAMES N.

1989   *American exodus: The Dust Bowl migration and Okie culture in California.* New York: Oxford University Press.

GUARNIZO, LUIS EDUARDO

1997   The emergence of a transnational social formation and the mirage of return migration among Dominican transmigrants. *Identities* 4:281–322.

GÜMÜŞÇÜ, OSMAN

2004   Internal migrations in sixteenth-century Anatolia. *Journal of Historical Geography* 30.2:231–248.

GUYER, JANE

1981   Household and community in African studies. *African Studies Review* 24.2/3:87–137.

GYORY, ANDREW

1998   *Closing the gate: Race, politics, and the Chinese Exclusion Act.* Chapel Hill: University of North Carolina Press.

HA, WEI, JUNJIAN YI, AND JUNSEN ZHANG

2009   Inequality and internal migration in China: Evidence from village panel data. Human Development Reports, Research Paper 2009/27. United Nations Development Programme.

HAGAN, JACQUELINE, KARL ESCHBACH, AND NESTOR RODRIGUEZ

2008   U.S. deportation policy, family separation, and circular migration. *International Migration Review* 42.1:64–88.

HAHN, STEVEN

2003   *A nation under our feet: Black political struggles in the rural South, from slavery to the Great Migration.* Cambridge, MA: Belknap Press of Harvard University Press.

HAMMAR, TOMAS, AND KRISTOF TAMAS

1997   Why do people go or stay? In *International migration, immobility, and development: Multidisciplinary perspectives*, ed. T. Hammar, G. Brochmann, K. Tamas, and T. Faist, 1–20. New York: Berg.

HAMMERTON, A. JAMES

2004   Gender and migration. In *Gender and empire*, ed. P. Levine, 156–180. New York: Oxford University Press.

HANEY, JANE B.

1979   Formal and informal labor recruitment mechanisms: Stages in Mexican migration into mid-Michigan agriculture. In *Migration across frontiers: Mexico and the United States*, ed. F. Camara and R. Van Kemper, 141–150. Contributions of the Latin American Anthropology Group 3. Albany: State University of New York.

HANNERZ, ULF

1996   *Transnational connections.* New York: Routledge.

HANSEN, METTE HALSKOV

2005   *Frontier people: Han settlers in minority areas of China.* Vancouver: University of British Columbia Press.

HARDING, LUKE, STEVEN MORRIS, AND LAURA SMITH

2005   GPs fear "flying doctors" crisis. *The Guardian.* http://www.guardian.co.uk/uk/2005/jun/17/germany.society.

HARM, C. M.

1985   Rural transformation on the east Black Sea coast of Turkey: A note on Keyder. *Journal of Peasant Studies* 12.4:101–110.

HARZIG, CHRISTIANE

2006   Domestics of the world (unite?): Labor migration systems and personal trajectories of household workers in historical and global perspectives. *Journal of American Ethnic History* 25.2–3:48–73.

HASHIM, IMAN

2007   Independent child migration and education in Ghana. *Development and Change* 38.5:911–931.

HE, CANFEI F., AND P. GOBER

2003   Gendering interprovincial migration in China. *International Migration Review* 37.4:1220–1251.

HERNANDEZ, ESTER, AND SUSAN BIBLER COUTIN

2006   Remitting subjects: Migrants, money, and states. *Economy and Society* 35.2:185–208.

HERNÁNDEZ DÍAZ, JORGE, ED.

2007   *Ciudadanías diferenciadas en un estado multicultural: Los usos y costumbres en Oaxaca.* Mexico, D.F.: Siglo XXI Editores: Universidad Autonoma Benito Juarez de Oaxaca.

HEYMAN, JOSIAH

2007   Environmental issues at the U.S.-Mexican border and the unequal territorialization of value. In *Rethinking environmental history: World-system history and global environmental change,* ed. A. Hornborg, J. R. McNeill, and J. Martinez-Alier, 327–344. Lanham: AltaMira.

HEYMANN, JODY, ET AL.

2009   The impact of migration on the well-being of transnational families: New data from sending communities in Mexico. *Community, Work, and Family* 12.1:91–103.

HILDEBRANDT, NICOLE, AND DAVID J. MCKENZIE

2006   The effects of migration on child health in Mexico. *Economia* 6.1:257–290.

HIRABAYASHI, LANE R.

1994   Mountain Zapotec migrants and forms of capital. *Political and Legal Anthropology Review* 17.2:105–116.

HIRSCHFELD, GERHARD

1984   *Exile in Great Britain: Refugees from Hitler's Germany.* Atlantic Highlands, NJ: Humanities Press.

HOGGART, KEITH, AND CRISTÓBAL MENDOZA

2000   African immigrant workers in Spanish agriculture. CCIS Working Papers, No. 2. San Diego: University of California, San Diego.

HONDAGNEU-SOTELO, PIERRETTE
1994   Family and community in the migration of Mexican undocumented immigrant women. In *Ethnic women: A multiple status reality*, ed. V. Demos and
M. T. Segal, 173–185. Dix Hills, NY: General Hall.

HORSTMANN, ALEXANDER, AND REED L. WADLEY, EDS.
2006   *Centering the margin: Agency and narrative in the southeast Asian borderlands.*
New York: Berghahn Books.

ICDUYGU, AHMET, AND IBRAHIM SIRKECI
1998   Changing dynamics of the migratory regime between Turkey and Arab
countries. *Turkish Journal of Population Studies* 20:3–16.

ICDUYGU, AHMET, IBRAHIM SIRKECI, AND GÜLNUR MURADOGLU
2001   Socio-economic development and international migration: A Turkish
study. *International Migration* 39.4:39–61.

ILLES, SANDOR
2005   Elderly immigration to Hungary. *Migration Letters* 2.2:164–169.

INEGI (EL INSTITUTO NACIONAL DE ESTADÍSTICA Y GEOGRAFÍA)
2008   Información estadística: Oaxaca. http://www.inegi.org.mx/inegi/de
fault.aspx?s=est&c=6990&e=20&i=.

INSTRAW (INTERNATIONAL RESEARCH AND TRAINING INSTITUTE FOR THE
ADVANCEMENT OF WOMEN)
2007   The feminization of international labor migration, gender, remittances,
and development. Working Paper 1. Santo Domingo: UN-INSTRAW.
www.un-instraw.org.

ISAAC, JULIUS
1947   *Economics of migration.* London: K. Paul, Trench, Trubner, and Co.

ITZIGSOHN, JOSÉ, ET AL.
1999   Mapping Dominican transnationalism: Narrow and broad transnational
practices. *Ethnic and Racial Studies* 22.2:316–339.

JENNY, R. K.
1984   The changing character of contemporary migration. *International Migration* 22.4:388–398.

JHA, SHIKHA, GUNTUR SUGIYARTO, AND CARLOS VARGAS-SILVA
2010   The global crisis and the impact on remittances to developing Asia. *Global
Economic Review* 39.1:59–82.

JORDAN, PETER
2006   Tourism and EU enlargement: A central European perspective. In *Tourism in the new Europe*, ed. D. R. Hall, M. K. Smith, and B. Marciszewska,
65–79. Wallingford: CABI Publishing.

KALHAN, ANIL

2010 Rethinking immigration detention. *Columbia Law Review Sidebar* 110/ Drexel University Earle Mack School of Law Research Paper No. 1556867.

KANDEL, WILLIAM, AND GRACE KAO

2000 Shifting orientations: How U.S. labor migration affects children's aspirations in Mexican migrant communities. *Social Science Quarterly* 81.1:16.

KAPTEIJNS, LIDWIEN, AND MARYAN OMAR ALI

2001 "Come back safely": Laments about labor migration in Somali love songs. *Northeast African Studies* 8.3:33–45.

KASHIWAZAKI, CHIKAKO

2005 *Japan's resilient demand for foreign workers*. Washington, DC: Migration Policy Institute.

KEARNEY, MICHAEL

1996 *Reconceptualizing the peasantry: Anthropology in global perspective*. Boulder: Westview.

KEMPADOO, KAMALA, AND JO DOEZEMA

1998 *Global sex workers: Rights, resistance, and redefinition*. New York: Routledge.

KENNEDY, ELIZABETH T.

2002 An analysis of risk perceptions: Understanding beneficiaries' concerns in sustainable development activities. In *Economic development: An anthropological approach*, ed. J. Cohen and N. Dannhaeuser, 137–160. Walnut Creek, CA: AltaMira Press.

KING, RUSSELL, AND JOHN CONNELL

1999 *Small worlds, global lives: Islands and migration*. London: Pinter.

KING, STEVEN

1997 Migrants on the margin? Mobility, integration, and occupations in the West Riding, 1650–1820. *Journal of Historical Geography* 23.3:284–303.

KINGMA, MIREILLE

2005 *Nurses on the move: Migration and the global health care economy*. Ithaca: Cornell University Press.

KINNAIRD, BOB

1999 Working holiday makers: More than tourists—Implications of the report of the Joint Standing Committee on Migration. *People and Place* 7.1:39–52.

KINOTI, KATHAMBI

2006 Women, remittances, and development. In *Resource Net Friday File*, issue 297. Toronto: Association for Women's Rights in Development.

KITIARSA, PATTANA

2008 Thai migrants in Singapore: State, intimacy, and desire. *Gender, Place, and Culture* 15.6:595–610.

KOC, ISMET, AND ISIL ONAN
2004   International migrants' remittances and welfare status of the left-behind families in Turkey. *International Migration Review* 38.1:78–112.

KOCH, ANDREA
1989   *Zapoteca migrants: The scheme of a transnational lifestyle.* M.A. thesis, University of Amsterdam.

KOENIG, DOLORES
2005   Multilocality and social stratification in Kita, Mali. In *Migration and economy: Global and local dynamics*, ed. L. Trager, 77–102. Lanham: AltaMira.

KONSTANTINOV, YULIAN
1996   Patterns of reinterpretation: Trader-tourism in the Balkans (Bulgaria) as a picaresque metaphorical enactment of post-totalitarianism. *American Ethnologist* 23.4:762–782.

KOSER, KHALID, AND NICHOLAS VAN HEAR
2003   Asylum migration and implications for countries of origin. UNU-WIDER Discussion Paper 2003/20. Helsinki: World Institute for Development Economics Research.

KRALER, ALBERT, AND KARIN SOHLER
2007   Austria. In *European immigration: A sourcebook*, ed. A. Triandafyllidou and R. Gropas, 19–31. Aldershot: Ashgate.

KULIKOFF, ALLAN
1992   *The agrarian origins of American capitalism.* Charlottesville: University Press of Virginia.

LADEK, DANA GRABER
2007   Iraq displacement: 2007 year in review. Geneva: International Organization for Migration. http://www.iom.int/jahia/webdav/shared/shared/mainsite/media/docs/reports/2007_year_in_review.pdf.

LAUBY, JENNIFER, AND ODED STARK
1987   Individual migration as a family strategy: Young women in the Philippines. Discussion Paper 35. Cambridge: Harvard University, Migration and Development Program.

LAVENEX, SANDRA
2001   *The Europeanisation of refugee policies: Between human rights and internal security.* Aldershot: Ashgate.

LEE, JOSEPHINE TSUI YUEH
2007   *New York City's Chinese community.* Charleston, SC: Arcadia.

LEPPAKARI, MARIA K.
2008   Religious tourism and pilgrimage management: An international perspective. *Annals of Tourism Research* 35.2:611–612.

LEVITT, PEGGY

1998   Social remittances: Migration-driven local-level forms of cultural diffu-
        sion. *International Migration Review* 32.4:926–948.

2001   *The transnational villagers*. Berkeley: University of California Press.

LEY, DAVID, AND AUDREY KOBAYASHI

2005   Back to Hong Kong: Return migration or transnational sojourn? *Global
        Networks* 5.2:111–127.

LIANG, ZAI, YIU POR CHEN, AND YANMIN GU

2002   Rural industrialization and internal migration in China. *Urban Studies*
        39.12:2175–2188.

LIVINGSTON, GRETCHEN

2006   Gender, job searching, and employment outcomes among Mexican im-
        migrants. *Population Research and Policy Review* 25.1:43–66.

LOZANO ASCENCIO, FERNANDO

1993   *Bringing it back home: Remittances to Mexico from migrant workers in the United
        States*. Trans. A. Yáñez. San Diego: Center for U.S.-Mexican Studies,
        UCSD.

LUCAS, ROBERT E.

2004   Life earnings and rural–urban migration. *Journal of Political Economy*
        112.1:S29–S59.

LUEBKE, FREDERICK C.

1999   *Germans in the New World: Essays in the history of immigration*. Urbana: Uni-
        versity of Illinois Press.

LUTHRA, RENEE REICHL

2009   Temporary immigrants in a high-skilled labour market: A study of
        H-1Bs. *Journal of Ethnic and Migration Studies* 35.2:227–250.

LYONS, GLENN, AND KIRON CHATTERJEE

2008   A human perspective on the daily commute: Costs, benefits, and trade-
        offs. *Transport Reviews* 28.2:181–198.

MAHLER, SARAH

1995   *America dreaming: Immigrant life on the margins*. Princeton: Princeton Uni-
        versity Press.

MANNING, CHRIS

2002   Structural change, economic crisis, and international labour migration in
        East Asia. *World Economy* 25.3:359–385.

MANNING, PATRICK

2005   *Migration in world history*. New York: Routledge.

MARCELLI, ENRICO A., AND B. LINDSAY LOWELL

2005   Transnational twist: Pecuniary remittances and the socioeconomic integration of authorized and unauthorized Mexican immigrants in Los Angeles County. *International Migration Review* 39.1:69–102.

MARTIN, PHILIP
2002   Mexican workers and U.S. agriculture: The revolving door. *International Migration Review* 36.4:1124–1142.

MARTIN, PHILIP, ELIZABETH MIDGLEY, AND MICHAEL S. TEITELBAUM
2002   Migration and development: Whither the Dominican Republic and Haiti? *International Migration Review* 36.2:570–592.

MASSEY, DOUGLAS S.
1990   Social structure, household strategies, and the cumulative causation of migration. *Population Index* 56.1:3–26.
1999   Why does immigration occur? A theoretical synthesis. In *The handbook of international migration: The American experience*, ed. C. Hirschman, J. DeWind, and P. Kasinitz, 34–52. New York: Russell Sage Foundation.

MASSEY, DOUGLAS S., ET AL.
1998   *Worlds in motion: Understanding international migration at the end of the millennium.* New York: Oxford University Press.

MASSEY, DOUGLAS S., AND F. GARCIA
1987   The social process of international migration. *Science* 237:733–738.

MASSEY, DOUGLAS S., LUIN GOLDRING, AND JORGE DURAND
1994   Continuities in transnational migration: An analysis of nineteen Mexican communities. *American Journal of Sociology* 99.6:1492–1533.

MASTERSON, DANIEL M., AND SAYAKA FUNADA-CLASSEN
2004   *The Japanese in Latin America.* Urbana: University of Illinois Press.

MCADAM, JANE
2008   *Forced migration, human rights, and security.* Oxford: Hart.

MCGHEE, DEREK
2003   Queer strangers: lesbian and gay refugees. *Feminist Review* 73.1:145–147.

MENCHACA, MARTHA
1995   *The Mexican outsiders: A community history of marginalization and discrimination in California.* Austin: University of Texas Press.

MIERA, FRAUKE
2008   Long-term residents and commuters: Change of patterns in migration from Poland to Germany. *Journal of Immigrant and Refugee Studies* 6.3:297–311.

MILLARD, ANN V., AND JORGE CHAPA
2004   *Apple pie and enchiladas.* Austin: University of Texas Press.

MINTZ, SIDNEY W.
1985   *Sweetness and power: The place of sugar in modern history.* New York: Viking.

MITTELMAN, JAMES H.

2000   *The globalization syndrome: Transformation and resistance.* Princeton: Princeton University Press.

MODEL, SUZANNE, AND LANG LIN

2002   The cost of not being Christian: Hindus, Sikhs, and Muslims in Britain and Canada. *International Migration Review* 36.4:1061–1092.

MOERMAN, D. MAX, AND MARTIN COLLCUTT

2008   Localizing paradise: Kumano pilgrimage and the religious landscape of premodern Japan. *Harvard Journal of Asiatic Studies* 68.1:176.

MONTO, ALEXANDER

1994   *The roots of Mexican labor migration.* Westport: Praeger.

MOONEY, ERIN

2005   The concept of internal displacement and the case for internally displaced persons as a category of concern. *Refugee Survey Quarterly* 24.3:9–26.

MOOREHEAD, CAROLINE

2005   *Human cargo: A journey among refugees.* New York: Holt.

MORAN-TAYLOR, MICHELLE J.

2008   When mothers and fathers migrate north: Caretakers, children, and child rearing in Guatemala. *Latin American Perspectives* 35.4:79–95.

MÖRNER, MAGNUS, AND HAROLD SIMS

1985   *Adventurers and proletarians: The story of migrants in Latin America.* Pittsburgh: University of Pittsburgh Press and UNESCO.

MORTIMER, MAJLINDA, AND ANCA TOADER

2005   Blood feuds blight Albanian lives. BBC News, Shkodra, Albania. http://news.bbc.co.uk/1/hi/world/europe/4273020.stm.

MOSES, JONATHON W., AND BJØRN LETNES

2003   If people were money: Estimating the potential gains from increased international migration. UNU-WIDER Discussion Paper 2003/41. Helsinki: World Institute for Development Economics Research.

MUELLBAUER, JOHN, AND GAVIN CAMERON

1998   The housing market and regional commuting and migration choices. www.cepr.org/pubs/dps/DP1945.asp.

MUTLU, SERVET

1996   Ethnic Kurds in Turkey: A demographic study. *International Journal of Middle East Studies* 28.4:517–541.

MYERSON, REBECCA, ET AL.

2010   Home and away: Chinese migrant workers between two worlds. *Sociological Review* 58.1:26–44.

NADEAU, KATHLEEN
2007   A maid in servitude: Filipino domestic workers in the Middle East. *Migration Letters* 4.1:15–27.

NAEGELE, JOLYON
2001   Albania: Blood feuds—Revenge makes fear, isolation a way of life. Radio Free Europe, 12 Oct. 2001. http://www.rferl.org/articleprint view/1097703.html.

NANGENGAST, CAROLE, RUDOLFO STAVENHAGEN, AND MICHAEL KEARNEY
1992   *Human rights and indigenous workers: The Mixtecs in Mexico and the United States.* San Diego: Center for U.S.-Mexican Studies.

NELL, LIZA M.
2004   Conceptualising the emergence of immigrants' transnational communities. *Migration Letters* 1.1:50–56.

NETTING, ROBERT MCC., ED.
1993   *Smallholders, householders: Farm families and the ecology of intensive, sustainable agriculture.* Stanford: Stanford University Press.

NETTING, ROBERT MCC., RICHARD WILK, AND ERIC ARNOULD, EDS.
1984   *Households: Comparative and historical studies of the domestic group.* Berkeley: University of California Press.

NIELSEN, THOMAS ALEXANDER SICK, AND HENRIK HARDER HOVGESEN
2008   Exploratory mapping of commuter flows in England and Wales. *Journal of Transport Geography* 16.2:90.

NOLIN, CATHERINE
2006   *Transnational ruptures: Gender and forced migration.* Aldershot: Ashgate.

O'CONNELL, PAUL G. J.
1997   Migration under uncertainty: "Try your luck" or "Wait and see." *Journal of Regional Science* 37.2:331–347.

OECD (ORGANIZATION FOR ECONOMIC COOPERATION AND DEVELOPMENT)
2005   Migration, remittances, and development. Paris: OECD Publications.

ONDIAK, NATALIE, AND OMER ISMAIL
2009   Darfur: A way of life lost. *Forced Migration Review* 33:27.

OROPESA, R. S., AND NANCY S. LANDALE
1997   Immigrant legacies: Ethnicity, generation, and children's familial and economic lives. *Social Science Quarterly* 78.2:399–416.

OROZCO, MANUEL
2002   Latino hometown associations as agents of development in Latin America. In *Sending money home: Hispanic remittances and community development*, ed. R. O. de la Garza and B. L. Lowell, 85–99. Lanham: Rowman and Littlefield.

ORUC, NERMIN

2009   Self-selection in conflict-induced migration: Micro evidence from Bosnia. Vienna: Vienna Institute for International Economic Studies. http://www.wiiw.ac.at/balkan/files/wiiw_GDN_SEE_Oruc09.pdf.

OSELLA, FILIPPO, AND CAROLINE OSELLA

2000   Migration, money, and masculinity in Kerala. *Journal of the Royal Anthropological Institute* (n.s.) 6.1:117–133.

OZBEKMEZCI, SULE, AND SARE SAHIL

2004   Housing style and life unit of the seasonal agricultural workers at Cukurova zone. *Journal of the Faculty of Engineering and Architecture of Gazi University* 19.4:375–391.

PAERREGAARD, KARSTEN

2008   *Peruvians dispersed: A global ethnography of migration.* Lanham: Rowman and Littlefield.

PANG, CHIN LIN

2007   Chinese migration and the case of Belgium. In *Migration in a New Europe: People, borders, and trajectories,* ed. T. van Naerssen and M. van der Velde, 87–109. Rome: Societa Geografica Italiana.

PANTOJA, ADRIAN D.

2005   Transnational ties and immigrant political incorporation: The case of Dominicans in Washington Heights, New York. *International Migration* 43.4:123–146.

PARREÑAS, RHACEL

2005   Long-distance intimacy: Class, gender, and intergenerational relations between mothers and children in Filipino transnational families. *Global Networks* 5.4:317–336.

PARSONS, TALCOTT

1954   *Essays in sociological theory.* Glencoe, IL: Free Press.

PENNARTZ, PAUL. J., AND ANKE NIEHOF

1999   *The domestic domain: Chances, choices, and strategies of family households.* Aldershot: Ashgate.

PLAZA, ROSIO CORDOVA

2007   Sexuality and gender in transnational spaces: Realignments in rural Veracruz families due to international migration. *Social Text* 25.3:37–55.

POJMANN, WENDY

2007   Organizing women migrants: The Filipino and Cape Verdean women's associations in Rome. *Migration Letters* 4.1:15–27.

POOLEY, COLIN G., AND IAN D. WHYTE, EDS.

1991   *Migrants, emigrants, and immigrants: A social history of migration.* New York: Routledge.

PORTES, ALEJANDRO
2007   Migration, development, and segmented assimilation: A conceptual re-
       view of the evidence. *Annals of the American Academy of Political and Social
       Science* 610.1:73–97.

PORTES, ALEJANDRO, AND L. E. GUARNIZO
1991   Tropical capitalists: U.S.-bound immigration and small-enterprise de-
       velopment in the Dominican Republic. In *Migration, remittances, and
       small business development: Mexico and Caribbean basin countries*, ed. S. Diaz-
       Briquets and S. Weintraub, 101–131. Boulder: Westview.

PORTES, ALEJANDRO, AND RUBÉN G. RUMBAUT
1996   *Immigrant America: A portrait.* Berkeley: University of California Press.

POSTLES, DAVID
2000   Migration and mobility in a less mature economy: English internal mi-
       gration, c. 1200–1350. *Social History* 25.3:285–299.

PRICE, MARIE
1994   Hands for the coffee: Migrants and western Venezuela's coffee produc-
       tion, 1870–1930. *Journal of Historical Geography* 20.1:62–80.

PRIES, LUDGER
1999   New migration in transnational space. In *Migration and transnational social
       spaces*, ed. L. Pries, 1–35. Aldershot: Ashgate.

QUIRK, JOEL
2007   Trafficked into slavery. *Journal of Human Rights* 6.2:181–207.

RASMUSSEN, JANET ELAINE
1993   *New land, new lives: Scandinavian immigrants to the Pacific Northwest.* North-
       field, MN: Norwegian-American Historical Association.

RATHA, DILIP
2007   Leveraging remittances for development. Policy brief, June. Washington,
       DC: Migration Policy Institute. http://www.migrationpolicy.org/pubs/
       MigDevPB_062507.pdf.

RATHA, DILIP, AND S. MOHAPATRA
2009   Revised outlook for remittance flows, 2009–2011: Remittances expected
       to fall by 7–10 percent in 2009. Migration and Development Briefs. Mi-
       gration and Remittances Team, Development Prospects Group, World
       Bank. http://siteresources.worldbank.org/INTPROSPECTS/Resources/
       334934-1110315015165/Migration&DevelopmentBrief10.pdf.

RATHA, DILIP, AND WILLIAM SHAW
2007   South–south migration and remittances. World Bank Working Paper 102.
       Washington, DC: World Bank.

RAVENSTEIN, ERNEST GEORGE
1889   The laws of migration. *Journal of the Royal Statistical Society* 52.2:241–301.

REGETS, M.
2008   Evolving markets: Adapting to the new high-skilled migration. *Harvard International Review* 30.3:62–67.

REICHERT, JOSHUA
1981   The migrant syndrome: Seasonal U.S. wage labor and rural development in central Mexico. *Human Organization* 40.1:56–66.

RENKOW, MITCH, AND DALE HOOVER
2000   Commuting, migration, and rural–urban population dynamics. *Journal of Regional Science* 40.2:261–287.

RIOS, BERNARDO
2008   *Torneo transnacional: Shooting hoops in Oaxacalifornia.* Columbus: PAST Foundation.

RIVERA-SALGADO, GASPAR
1999   Mixtec activism in Oaxacalifornia. *American Behavioral Scientist* 42.9: 1439–1458.
2000   Transnational political strategies: The case of Mexican indigenous migrants. In *Immigration research for a new century*, ed. N. Foner, R. G. Rumbaut, and S. J. Gold, 134–156. New York: Russell Sage Foundation.

RIVERA-SALGADO, GASPAR, AND LUIS ESCALA RABANDAN
2004   Collective identity and organizational strategies of indigenous and mestizo Mexican migrants. In *Indigenous Mexican migrants in the United States*, ed. J. Fox and G. Rivera-Salgado, 145–178. San Diego: University of California Press, the Center for U.S.-Mexican Studies, and the Center for Comparative Immigration Studies.

ROOSEVELT, THEODORE
1918   A square deal for all Americans. In *Kansas City Star*.

ROSE, SUSAN, AND ROBERT SHAW
2008   The gamble: Circular Mexican migration and the return on remittances. *Mexican Studies/Estudios Mexicanos* 24.1:79–111.

ROTHERMUND, DIETMAR
1996   *The global impact of the Great Depression, 1929-1939.* London: Routledge.

ROUSE, ROGER
1991   Mexican migration and the social space of postmodernism. *Diaspora* 1.1:8–23.

RUBENSTEIN, HYMIE
1982   The impact of remittances in the rural English-speaking Caribbean: Notes on the literature. In *Return migration and remittances: Developing a Caribbean perspective*, ed. W. F. Stinner, K. De Albuquerque, and R. S. Bryce-Laporte, 237–266. RIIES Occasional Papers 3. Washington, DC: Research Institute on Immigration and Ethnic Studies, Smithsonian Institution.

RUNSTEN, DAVID, AND MICHAEL KEARNEY

1994   *A survey of Oaxacan village networks in California agriculture.* Davis: California Institute for Rural Studies.

RYAN, LOUISE, ET AL.

2009   Family strategies and transnational migration: Recent Polish migrants in London. *Journal of Ethnic and Migration Studies* 35.1:61–77.

SAFRIAN, HANS

2001   Expediting expropriation and expulsion: The impact of the "Vienna Model" on anti-Jewish policies in Nazi Germany, 1938. *Peace Research Abstracts* 38.4:451–600.

SANCHEZ, NYDIA DELHI MATA

2007   *Migración, desarrollo y turismo nostálgico en San Francisco Cajonos, 1990-2005.* Master's thesis. Oaxaca, Mexico: Instituto Tecnologico de Oaxaca.

SANTIAGO-IRIZARRY, VILMA

2008   Transnationalism and migration: Locating sociocultural practices among Mexican immigrants in the United States. *Reviews in Anthropology* 37.1:16–40.

SANTOS, CÂNDIDA RIBEIRO

2007   *Panorama da migração dos municípios baianos em 1995-2000.* Salvador, Bahia: SEI.

SASSEN, SASKIA

1998   *Globalization and its discontents.* New York: New Press.

SCHANO, RICHARD

2008   A "balanced approach" to airport marketing: The impact of low-cost airlines on tourism in Salzburg. *Journal of Airport Management* 3.1:54–61.

SCHEURLE, J., AND R. SEYDEL

2000   A model of student migration. *International Journal of Bifurcation and Chaos* 10:477–480.

SCHMALZBAUER, LEAH

2008   Family divided: The class formation of Honduran transnational families. *Global Networks* 8.3:329–346.

SCHNEIDER, ARND

2000   *Futures lost: Nostalgia and identity among Italian immigrants in Argentina.* New York: Lang.

SCHWARTZMAN, KATHLEEN

2009   The role of labor struggle in the shifting ethnic composition of labor markets. *Labor Studies Journal* 34.2:189–218.

SCOTT, SAM, AND KIM H. CARTLEDGE

2009   Migrant assimilation in Europe: A transnational family affair. *International Migration Review* 43.1:60–89.

SCULLION, HUGH, DAVID G. COLLINGS, AND PATRICK GUNNIGLE
2007   International human resource management in the twenty-first century: Emerging themes and contemporary debates. *Human Resource Management Journal* 17.4:309–319.

SEMYONOV, MOSHE, AND ANASTASIA GORODZEISKY
2005   Labor migration, remittances, and household income: A comparison between Filipino and Filipina overseas workers. *International Migration Review* 39.1:45–68.
2008   Labor migration, remittances, and economic well-being of households in the Philippines. *Population Research and Policy Review* 27.5:619–637.

SHLOMOWITZ, RALPH
1990   *The Latin American engache system: A comment on brass.* Bedford Park: Flinders University of South Australia.

SILLS, STEPHEN J.
2007   Philippine labour migration to Taiwan: Social, political, demographic, and economic dimensions. *Migration Letters* 4.1:1–14.

SINGER, AUDREY, AND DOUGLAS S. MASSEY
1998   The social process of undocumented border crossing among Mexican migrants. *International Migration Review* 32.3:561–592.

SIRKECI, IBRAHIM
2000   Exploring the Kurdish population in the Turkish context. *GENUS: International Journal of Demography* 56.1–2:149–179.
2005   War in Iraq: Environment of insecurity and international migration. *International Migration* 43.4:197–214.
2006a   *The environment of insecurity in Turkey and the emigration of Turkish Kurds to Germany.* Lewiston, NY: Edwin Mellen Press.
2006b   Ethnic conflict, wars, and international migration of Turkmen: Evidence from Iraq. *Migration Letters* 3.1:31–42.
2009   Transnational mobility and conflict. *Migration Letters* 6.1:3–14.

SIRKECI, IBRAHIM, JEFFREY COHEN, AND NERIMAN CAN
Forthcoming   *Türkiye'deki yurtdışı doğumluların yurtiçi göç hareketleri ya da göçmenlerin içgöçü* [Internal migration of the foreign-born in Turkey]. Ankara: Sosyolojik Araştırmalar Dergisi [Sociological Association of Turkey].

SKELDON, RONALD
2008   International migration as a tool in development policy: A passing phase? *Population and Development Review* 34.1:1–18.

SKOP, EMILY, ET AL.
2006   Chain migration and residential segregation of internal migrants in the metropolitan area of São Paulo, Brazil. *Urban Geography* 27.5:397–421.

SMITH, MARRISA

2007   Urban expansion in Oaxaca, Mexico: Research on the fringe. *Yearbook of the Association of Pacific Coast Geographers* 69:88–100.

SMITH, ROBERT C.

2006   *Mexican New York: Transnational lives of new immigrants.* Berkeley: University of California Press.

STAFFON, BEATRIZ, PAOLA LÓPEZ, AND ANAILY CASTELLANOS

2006   Migración indígena, prácticas comunitarias y costumbres de participación. In *El programa 3 × 1 para migrantes en Oaxaca*, ed. R. Fernández de Castro et al., 197–222. Mexico: Instituto Tecnológico Autónomo de México/Universidad Autónoma de Zacatecas/Miguel Ángel Porrúa.

STARK, ODED, ED.

1986   *Migration theory, human capital, and development.* Greenwich, CT: JAI Press.

1991   Migration in LDCs: Risk, remittances, and the family. *Finance and Development* 28.4:39–41.

STARK, ODED, AND J. EDWARD TAYLOR

1989   Relative deprivation and international migration. *Demography* 26.1:1–14.

STARK, ODED, AND YOU QIANG WANG

2002   *Migration dynamics.* Economics series 112. Vienna: Institute for Advanced Studies.

STAVE, BRUCE M., JOHN F. SUTHERLAND, AND ALDO SALERNO

1994   *From the Old Country: An oral history of European migration to America.* New York: Twayne.

STRAND, ARNE, ASTRI SUHRKE, AND KRISTIAN BERG HARPVIKEN

2004   *Afghan refugees in Iran: From refugee emergency to migration management.* Oslo: PRIO International Peach Research Institute. http://www.cmi.no/pdf/?file=/afghanistan/doc/CMI-PRIO-AfghanRefugeesInIran.pdf.

STYAN, DAVID

2007   The security of Africans beyond borders: Migration, remittances, and London's transnational entrepreneurs. *International Affairs* 83.6:1171–1191.

SUZUKI, TAKU

2006   Becoming "Japanese" in Bolivia: Okinawan-Bolivian trans(national) formations in Colonia Okinawa. *Identities: Global Studies in Culture and Power* 13:455–581.

TANNER, ARNO

2005   *Emigration, brain drain, and development: The case of sub-Saharan Africa.* Helsinki: East-West Books/Migration Policy Institute.

TAYLOR, J. EDWARD, ET AL.

1996   International migration and national development. *Population Index* 62.2:181–212.

2005   Remittances, inequality, and poverty: Evidence from rural Mexico. Working Paper 05-003. Davis, CA: Department of Agricultural and Resource Economics, University of California, Davis.

TAYLOR, J. EDWARD, S. ROZELLE, AND A. DE BRAUW
2003   Migration and incomes in source communities: A new economics of migration perspective from China. *Economic Development and Cultural Change* 52.1:75–101.

TAYLOR, J. EDWARD, AND T. J. WYATT
1996   The shadow value of migrant remittances, income, and inequality in a household-farm economy. *Journal of Development Studies* 32.6:899–912.

TÉLLEZ, MARÍA EUGENIA ANGUIANO
2008   Chiapas: Territorio de inmigración, emigración y tránsito migratorio. *Papeles de Población* 14 (56): 215–232.

TERRAZAS, AARON, AND JEANNE BATALOVA
2009   Frequently requested statistics on immigrants and immigration in the United States. Migration Policy Institute. http://www.migrationinformation.org/USFocus/print.cfm?ID=747.

THAPAR-BJÖRKERT, SURUCHI
2007   Conversations across borders: Men and honour violence in U.K. and Sweden. INTER: A European Cultural Studies Conference in Sweden, Advanced Cultural Studies Institute of Sweden (ACSIS), Norrköping, Sweden. Linköping University Electronic Press at www.ep.liu.se/ecp/025/.

TODARO, M. P.
1996   Income expectations, rural–urban migration, and employment in Africa. *International Labour Review/International Labour Office* 135.3–4:3–4.

TRIANDAFYLLIDOU, ANNA
2009   Sub-Saharan African immigrant activists in Europe: Transcultural capital and transcultural community building. *Ethnic and Racial Studies* 32.1:93–116.

TRISAL, NISHITA
2007   Those who remain: The survival and continued struggle of the Kashmiri pandit "non-migrants." *Journal of Immigrant and Refugee Studies* 5.3:99–114.

TURTON, DAVID
2003   Conceptualizing forced migration. Refugee Studies Centre Working Paper 12. Oxford: University of Oxford.

UNITED NATIONS (U.N.)
2006   International migration and development. General Assembly, 16th Session, Agenda Item 54 (c), Globalization and interdependence: International migration and development. New York: United Nations.

UNDP (UNITED NATIONS DEVELOPMENT PROGRAMME)
2005   Human Development Report. International cooperation at a crossroads: Aid, trade, and security in an unequal world. New York: United Nations Development Programme. http://hdr.undp.org/en/reports/global/hdr 2005/chapters/.

VAIOU, DINA, AND MARIA STRATIGAKI
2008   From "settlement" to "integration": Informal practices and social services for women migrants in Athens. *European Urban and Regional Studies* 15.2:119–131.

VALENTINE, GILL, DEBORAH SPORTON, AND KATRINE BANG NIELSEN
2009   Identities and belonging: A study of Somali refugee and asylum seekers living in the UK and Denmark. *Environment and Planning D: Society and Space* 27.2:234–250.

VANDEGRIFT, DARCIE
2008   "This isn't paradise—I work here": Global restructuring, the tourism industry, and women workers in Caribbean Costa Rica. *Gender and Society* 22.6:778–798.

VELAYUTHAM, SELVARAJ, AND AMANDA WISE
2005   Moral economics of a translocal village: Obligation and shame among South Indian transnational migrants. *Global Networks* 5.1:27–46.

VERTOVEC, STEVEN
2009   *Transnationalism.* London: Routledge.

VILLAFUERTE SOLÍS, DANIEL, AND MARÍA DEL CARMEN GARCÍA AGUILAR, EDS.
2008   *Migraciones en el sur de México y Centroamérica.* Tuxtla Gutiérrez, Chiapas, Mexico: Universidad de Ciencias y Artes de Chiapas y Miguel Ángel Porrúa.

VIQUEIRA, JUAN PEDRO
2008   Indios y Ladinos, arraigados y migrantes en Chiapas: Un esbozo de historia demográfica de larga duración. In *Migraciones en el sur de México y Centroamérica*, ed. D. Villafuerte Solís and M. C. García Aguilar, 275–322. Tuxtla Gutiérrez, Chiapas, Mexico: Universidad de Ciencias y Artes de Chiapas y Miguel Ángel Porrúa.

VIVAR, TÁSACUA
2009   La falta de remesas de dólares empieza a hacer crisis en el agro oaxaqueño. *Noticias en linea,* 8 Aug. 2009.

VOIGT-GRAF, CARMEN
2008   Migration and transnational families in Fiji: Comparing two ethnic groups. *International Migration* 46.4:15–40.

VRYER, MIEPJE A. DE

1989   Leaving, longing, and loving: A developmental perspective of migration. *Journal of American College Health* 38.2:75–80.

WAGNER, JONATHAN

2006   *A history of migration from Germany to Canada, 1850–1939.* Vancouver: University of British Columbia Press.

WALDINGER, ROGER, AND MICHAEL I. LICHTER

2003   *How the other half works: Immigration and the social organization of labor.* Berkeley: University of California Press.

WAREING, JOHN

1981   Migration to London and the transatlantic emigration of indentured servants, 1683–1775. *Journal of Historical Geography* 7.4:356–378.

WHITAKER, ROBERT C. SHANNON M. PHILLIPS, AND SEAN M. ORZOL

2006   Food insecurity and the risks of depression and anxiety in mothers and behavior problems in their preschool-aged children. *Pediatrics* 118: e859–e868.

WHO (WORLD HEALTH ORGANIZATION)

2005   *Health and migration: Bridging the gap.* Geneva: World Health Organization.

WILK, RICHARD R.

1989   Decision making and resource flows within the household: Beyond the black box. In *The household economy*, ed. R. R. Wilk, 23–54. Boulder: Westview.

1991   *Household ecology: Economic change and domestic life among the Kekchi Maya in Belize.* Tucson: University of Arizona Press.

2006   "But the young men don't want to farm anymore": Political ecology and consumer culture in Belize. In *Reimagining political ecology*, ed. A. Biersack and J. B. Greenberg, 149–170. Durham: Duke University Press.

WILLIAMS, A. M., V. BAL, AND D. KOLL

2001   Coming and going in Slovakia: International labour mobility in the Central European "buffer zone." *Environment and Planning A* 33.6:1101–1123.

WISE, AMANDA

2006   *Exile and return among the East Timorese.* Philadelphia: University of Pennsylvania Press.

WOLF, ERIC

1972   Ownership and political ecology. *Anthropological Quarterly* 45.3:201–205.

1982   *Europe and the people without history.* Berkeley: University of California Press.

WONG, M.

2006   The gendered politics of remittances in Ghanaian transnational families. *Economic Geography* 82.4:355–381.

WORLD BANK

2006   Global economic prospects, 2006: Economic implications of remittances and migration. Washington, DC: World Bank.

2009   World Bank Speak Out: Interview with Dilip Ratha on remittances. http://discuss.worldbank.org/content/interview/detail/9277/. In World Bank Speak Out: World Bank.

YAGHMAIAN, BEHZAD

2005   *Embracing the infidel: Stories of Muslim migrants on the journey west.* New York: Delacorte.

YANG, DEAN, AND CLAUDIA A. MARTÍNEZ

2006   Remittances and poverty in migrants' home areas: Evidence from the Philippines. In *International migration, remittances, and the brain drain*, ed. Ç. Özden and M. W. Schiff, e81–e122. Washington, DC: World Bank and Palgrave Macmillan.

YILDIRIM, MURAT, AND FUAT TAPAN

2008   29 yıldır süren 'öküz kavgası'nda barış [End of the age-old feud over an ox]. In *Sabah Gazetesi.* 19 Oct. 2008.

YUDINA, TATIANA

2005   Labour migration into Russia: The response of state and society. *Current Sociology* 53.4:583–606.

YUKSEKER, DENIZ

2007   Shuttling goods, weaving consumer tastes: Informal trade between Turkey and Russia. *International Journal of Urban and Regional Research* 31.1:60–72.

ZELINSKY, WILBUR

1971   The hypothesis of the mobility transition. *Geographical Review* 61.2: 219–249.

ZETTER, ROGER

2007   More labels, fewer refugees: Remaking the refugee label in an era of globalization. *Journal of Refugee Studies* 20.2:172–192.

ZHAO, YAOHUI

1999   Labor migration and earnings differences: The case of rural China. *Economic Development and Cultural Change* 47.4:767–782.

ZLOLNISKI, CHRISTIAN

2006   *Janitors, street vendors, and activists: The lives of Mexican immigrants in Silicon Valley.* Berkeley: University of California Press.

ZOLBERG, ARISTIDE R.

1999   Matters of state: Theorizing immigration policy. In *The handbook of international migration: The American experience*, ed. C. Hirschman, P. Kasinitz, and J. DeWind, 71–93. New York: Russell Sage Foundation.

INDEX

Iranians, 95

Iraq, 4, 47, 63, 72

Iraqis, 15

Ireland, 81

Irish, 39

Irish Famine, 39

Isaac, Julius, 71

Islam, 29, 51, 52, 62, 76. *See also* Muslims

ismakhen (ex-slaves), 103

Israel, 15

Italy, 61, 74, 81

Japan, 38; occupation of, 47; Okinawa, 81

Japanese, 81

jobs, 15, 22, 26, 27, 60, 75

job security, 108

Juarez, Benito, 31

kan davasi (blood feud), 108

Kanun (feuds), 108

Kashmiri, 87

Kennedy, John F., 114, 115

Kenya, 12, 85, 112

King, Steven, 40

Koenig, Dolores, 57

Koranic law, 29

Koser, Khalid, 105

Kurds, ix, x, 4, 12, 15, 34, 44, 63, 64, 80, 95; anti-Kurd, 24; Kurdish minority, 110; Turkish, 12, 24, 84

Kurdistan Workers Party, 84–85

labor: camps, 47; day, 100; markets, 21, 34, 53, 64; coerced/forced, 44; unskilled, 78

landed gentry, 57

landholders, 44, 80

Laotians, 4

Latin America, 44, 48, 59, 71, 72, 100. *See also individual countries*

Lebanon, 15, 18

Letnes, Bjorn, 101

Levitt, Peggy, 111

Los Angeles, California, 8, 9, 31, 82

low-wage work, 56, 78

Luxembourg, 5

Lyons, Glenn, 56

macro-level, x, xi; patterns, 38; processes, 21; trends, 16

Mali (Kita), 57

marriage/marital status, 22, 24, 25, 44, 98; and husbands, 15, 27, 41, 45, 77, 90, 123n2; unmarried movers, 22; and weddings, 4, 24, 103, 108

Massey, Douglas, xii, 26, 47

media: popular, 14; right-wing, 73

Mexican(s), xi, xii, 4, 8, 42, 45, 81, 84

Mexico, ix, 8, 14, 16, 18, 21, 26, 27, 36, 74, 75, 79, 83, 94, 95, 103; border of, with Texas, 121; Chiapas, 11, 60; Durango, 11; Guanajuato, 11; Jalisco, 11; Mexico City, 9, 43, 62; rural, 102, 105; Sierra Madre Occidental, 31; Zacatecas, 11. *See also* Oaxaca

Middle East, x, 23, 72, 74, 84. *See also individual countries*

migrants, xii, 4, 10, 12, 14, 20, 28, 80, 81, 102, 115; contemporary, 42; forced, 42, 71; future, 91; indentured, 42; internal, 101; Mexican, 89, 91; recruiting of, 31, 80, 98; skilled, 4, 9, 80, 105; unskilled, 4, 5, 79. *See also* migration; movers

migration, ix, xi, 1, 2, 9, 19, 32, 65, 90, 111; contemporary, 50; costs of, 69; critics of, 78; cross-border, 60; cultural effects of, 70; and decision making, 61; defined, 7; diversity and, 49; domestic, 60; early, 38; forced, 5, 45, 46, 47, 48; gender and, 64; global, 81; history of, 116; impacts of, 70; intensity, 54; internal, 53, 63; international, 63, 68, 70, 76, 86; linear-